GOSSIP, LIES, AND JUDGEMENT

Published by

AB Film Publishing

Whenever the plays are produced the following notice must appear on all programs, printing, and advertising for the play:

"Produced by special arrangements with
AB Film Publishing"

Due authorship credit must be given on all programs, printing and advertising for the plays.

Gay for Pay © 2019 Alan Baxter

Arlene's Descent © 2019 Sal Anzalone

Casting Stones © 2019 Alan Baxter

ISBN: 978-0-9971718-1-8

Cover Design by Thomas Romano, USA
Published by
AB Film Publishing
2021

AB Film Publishing

Foreword To Three Plays

Gay For Pay, Arlene's Descent and *Casting Stones* are contentious plays. In our daily lives, most of us go out of our way to avoid explosive, crass and bigoted people. But in plays such characters are fascinating to watch. Lead characters in these three plays are either bullies or victims, or pretend they are victims, when in fact, they are not. Subjects explored include homophobia, racism and transphobia-just to name a few. Readers/audiences may agree or disagree with the characters, but one certainty exists: all will be astounded by the climactic finales.

GAY FOR PAY

by Alan Baxter

SYNOPSIS

A San Francisco father, Justin Scott, finds out that his 19-year old son has probably run away from home, only to find out that he has become lost in the wilds of Montreal, Canada. When Scott arrives in the Quebecois city, he has an encounter with a film producer, Jack Hemmings, whom he had a strange relationship with in his California high school. This situation sets the stage for a clash of social relationships that lead into a climatic ending.

Gay for Pay was first dramatically read by actors at the SAGE Gay Center in New York City, during the fall of 2018. The response was very positive, and after a few revisions, the play was dramatically read by other companies here in New York, especially Genevieve Productions. Since then, this piece has been sought after by a few theaters outside New York who show a strong interest in having productions with Gay content. Thus the publication of this work.

Cast:

Bill, well- built Caucasian young man, age 19
Donny, well-built, Caucasian young man, age 19
Jack Hemmings, an ex-American film producer, age 47
Marie-Ann Cadieux, a young Canadian film student and intern, age 20
Justin Scott, an American psychologist and writer, age 48
JoAnn Scott, his wife, age 45

Note: **Even though the play takes place in both Montreal and San Francisco**, it only demands some sketchy sets which reflect the location and the times. Nudity can be used in parts, but it is certainly not mandatory.

GAY FOR PAY

ACT ONE

Scene One

Lounge Area of a small Film Studio in Montreal, Canada: Bill and Donny, two very sexy looking men, aged 19, step into the room, with only towels draped around their waist. They are obviously nude because they have just finished acting in a Gay porno film. Year: 1986

DONNY
Hey, dude, I hope I didn't hurt your ass that much.

BILL
I'm not a chicken.

(They embrace, a sort of street brother embrace.)

DONNY
Not bad as I thought it would be. Still, my first time. Pretty soon, we'll all be queers.

BILL
The directors tell bottoms to scream and yell. The viewers get off on that. "Give it to me... give it to me, man...Harder, harder!!"

(Bill mimics the exaggerated sound of an orgasm. They both laugh.)

DONNY

Hey, that's an awesome tattoo of a cross on your shoulder.

BILL

Like, I'm very Spiritually-minded--- not religious---but Spiritual

DONNY

That's groovy. I guess this video makes us very special.

BILL

We're just like movie stars. Except we go all the way. One dude recognized me. Thought I was that new actor Tom Cruise.

DONNY (looking at Bill's ass))

Yeah, Queer guys tell me they love being fucked. That is, if they are more of a bottom than a top. (laughing) That right?

BILL
Right.

(Suddenly Donny explodes with anger.)

DONNY

Tell anyone else about this, I'll kill ya.

BILL

Take a chill pill, man. It's just between us. Bitches don't watch this.

DONNY

Sorry.

                              BILL
Straight, right?

                              DONNY
How ya guess?

                              BILL
You seemed a bit uncomfortable at times. I
could tell there were moments when it was
difficult for you to get a hard-on.

                              DONNY
With all those damn cameras looking at me.

                              BILL
Like you can beat off in public.

                              DONNY
It was not my first time sucking cock. And
please don't tell no one about that.

                              BILL
So, you're not totally straight !! (teasing)

                              DONNY
When a bitch is not around, what else ye gonna do?

                              BILL
Look, I'm not that Gay. Maybe not that straight
either. Whatever cuts it. I know exactly how
you feel. But you still gotta be careful these
days. AIDS----that's a bummer.

                              DONNY
That's great that Ed made us wear condoms.
Nowadays we gotta do it. But, man, keepin' a
hard on. How d'ya do it?

BILL
I done a number of these pornos before, and the
only way I can get it up is when I fantasized
that I was doing it with Marie-Anne.
Course when I can't see her naked body that
well, I let Miguel or the fluffer finish it all
up.

DONNY
So why can't they let us fuck pussy?

BILL (holding up his hands)
The dough, man. Hey, you can do it if you like.
You only make good money when you do Gay.

DONNY
So I'm told. Now I think I'll be able to rent a
little apartment in Cote de Neiges. (American
pronunciation) But I need more money to buy a
car.

BILL
How ye get here?

DONNY
Not been for this dude that my ex- knew from
McGill, I never would been able to get away
from my old man in California.

BILL
Cali---Awesome.

DONNY
Yep, right north of San Francisco.

(Bill pauses for a moment.)

GAY FOR PAY   4

                    BILL
Figured you from the States. The accent. Why
Montreal?

                    DONNY
Heard there were lotta work for guys with our
build. More so than in Northern California,
believe it not.
But Montreal-- a beautiful city in its own
right. Yeah, kinda like San Francisco.
Also, my Mother. she was brought up in
Montreal.

                    BILL
Hey, so was my mum. She's originally from
Montreal.

                    DONNY
So, we're brothers. Give it here, man.

        (They both embrace.)

                    BILL
You probably have relatives here, right?

                    DONNY
Not really. She was really young when she left
here.

                    BILL
Same with my Mother.

        (There is a small pause.)

                    BILL
But, just don't tell too many other Quebecois
body builders that you're American.

DONNY

Why ?

BILL

Lot of them don't like Americans crossing the
border and taking jobs away from them. A lot of
them would like to make the easy money we're
making, stripping and doing porn.

DONNY

You don't sound Quebecois.

BILL(slapping him with a towel)

How do you know?

DONNY

I know I don't speak French that well. But
that's the good thing about Montreal. You can
get by on just English.

BILL

Yeah, and bad French. That's how I get around.

DONNY

You're American, too. Right?

BILL

Thumbed all the way from Chicago.

DONNY

That can be a trip.

BILL

Seriously, I gave two guys a blow job if I
could get enough to rent a car. And I did.
Drove all the way from Illinois. Like you,

lucky enough to have my driver's license
with me. When I arrived here, I also just
like you. (holding up the cash) Our little
salvation.

                    DONNY
How your girl friend feel about your doing
this.

                    BILL
My American woman? She would never know. We
broke up

                    DONNY
Same with me, even though we were together all
in Prep School.

                    BILL
But my new one in Montreal? Doesn't like it
at all. Course, it was my American one that
connected me to Marie-Ann.

                    DONNY
The one from St. Louis.

                    BILL
No, the one from where I originally came from.
Miles and miles from St. Louis.

                    DONNY
Which is ?

                    BILL
Clue you in some other time.

                    DONNY
Didn't mean to pry. Man.

                    BILL
Don't worry about it.

          DONNY (flexing his shoulders)
Gonna take me awhile to get used to this
Canadian winter and to this goddamn March.

                    BILL
Don't knock it, man. March is my birthday
month.

                    DONNY
Hey, a winter baby.

                    BILL
Bryan Cranston, Harry Bellefonte, ------

                    DONNY
Oh, yeah, I loved Harry Bellefonte-----

                    BILL
Desi Arnaz------

                    DONNY
What the fuck did he do?

                    BILL
Com'on, man. I Love Lucy !

                    DONNY
That's wild, man. Just like us. (pause) But
don't you wish you were doing what these guys
were doing?

                    BILL
No way. The first time I did this---- ecstatic.
Not even drugs could do what I achieved.

GAY FOR PAY

To take off all my clothes and make love in
front of the camera. A fantastic feeling of
liberation. Like sharing my naked self to the
rest of the world.

                    DONNY
Yeah, like I told Ed, I really wanted to do it,
but he had to give me condoms. As you said,
with AIDS, you have to be careful, real, real
careful. Also told me about the code-word.
I didn't tell him, but I wanted to be under
cocaine when I did it.

                    BILL
Speaking of AIDS, make sure you say stay away
from under Jacques-Cartier Bridge. Needles
everywhere.

                    DONNY
For real?

                    BILL
Even be careful of Park Champlain. If you find a
sugar-daddy, they'll rip you off of everything.

                    DONNY
Ain't it just the opposite.

                    BILL
Some guys up here have Mafia type guys working
for them. Just looking for the unsuspected new
guy. But that is very rare. People up here are
very nice. Montreal is probably the safest city
in North America.

                    DONNY
How easy is it to get a good fuck in Montreal?

I hear it's pretty wild here. You can do anything you want in this city.

                    BILL
Chicks here---- real feminists. They're not
even required to change their name when they
marry. It's the law. The only easy ones are the
sluts like us.

                    DONNY
I'll have to wait until I finish a few more
pornos.

                    BILL
Hey, if you want to make some quick cash, this
Friday---Vendredi—I can get you a good job
stripping, along with me. It's at Le 'Garage.
But this time it's all for the ladies. No fag
stuff.

                    DONNY
Great.

                    BILL
I'll connect you with Marie Anne. She's coming.

                    DONNY
Your girlfriend. Get outta here. I don't wanna
steal your woman

                    BILL
Nah, man. I told you. I'm on the "outs" with
Marie Anne. It's really over. We didn't hit it
off that well. I'm looking for someone else.

                    DONNY
But you said she was upset about the sexy

performances you do. How she's gonna feel about me?

                    BILL
Stripping don't bother her. Just the videos she gets upset about. She's afraid her friends all the way up in Lac St. Jean are going to see me. Like they know what I look like. But she'll love you. She digs young American guys.

        (Donny hugs Bill again.)

                    DONNY
Thanks, man. Here's to the next porno together.

(BLACK OUT)

Scene Two

Inside the Premier Film Production Central Office on the outskirts of Montreal. Jack Hemming, a handsome American man in his 40's is sitting at his desk, looking at financial numbers on his desk. Jack is also on the phone, arguing with an actor. In walks Marie Anne Cadieux, a young, very attractive girl about 20. She is an intern from Concordia College and is also Quebecois.

                    JACK
Fuck it what they do in the States. It's
different here……..
So take a hike, and finish that little shitty
job for Warner Bros.. We'll find someone else.

                    MARIE ANN
Alors, qu'est-ce qu'il voulait? The Palace
Versaille?

                    JACK
I hate Americans!!! And even that wouldn't have
made him happy.

                    MARIE ANNE
Why you angry at the French?

                    JACK
Don't get me wrong. The French sure give better
benefits, and you're affected over here in
Quebec. But it's like hell having to work it
into the budget.

                    MARIE ANNE
C'est la vie. Tout pour les employes.

                    JACK
Maybe I should have thought twice before
deciding to become a line producer. But years
ago I really needed the money.

                 MARIE ANNE
You have the same thing in the States. N' est-
ce pas?

                    JACK
IATSE doesn't ready get on us because of the
overtime. And extras? SAG allows them to get
peanuts for the same work that can last 20
hours more.

                 MARIE ANNE
Don't mean personal, but you never did tell me
why you left the States.

                    JACK
Now you're getting nosy, Marie

            MARIE ANNE (a bit embarrassed)
Sorry---sorry. Up here, we want to get to know
people too much.

                    JACK
Don't knock it. You have a great city here in
Montreal----a civilized city.

                 MARIE ANNE
The night life-----the show business
connections ?

                    JACK
Hey, prostitution is practically legal here...

                    MARIE ANNE
No it's not !!

                    JACK
No one getting shot after the fun's all over.
Everyone friendlier and more welcoming. No
annoying ring of the cash register. Everything
in the States has a price tag on it. Movies all
about the box office.

                    MARIE ANNE
That bad in the States?

                    JACK
Look at American politics, Ronald Reagan.
Politics is like a Hollywood movie. Hundreds of
guys are dying of AIDS, and Reagan's not doing
a goddamn thing about it.

                    MARIE ANNE
You been here ---- 10 years?

                    JACK
No, I keep telling people—15 years.

                    MARIE ANNE
Maybe people no understand you?

                    JACK
That's the trouble. I speak in French and
everybody responds to me In English.

                    MARIE ANNE
Mostly Anglo friends?

                    JACK

Just as many Quebecois friends. How do you think I got this job? Now you are getting personal. You're nosy. Prends plus de risques comme un homme americain?

MARIE ANNE
We interns can be stupid. You know that. But you say you had no boy friends now, so maybe you're a bit---- say-----bit-------lonely?

JACK
I don't do personal sex. It's all related to the money. I get my love kicks in massage parlors, by paying off young guys. And I mean young legal guys, with bubble-built asses. "Tes nuits d'amours"

MARIE ANNE
You men are all the same horny pigs !! Your bar for love is rooted in what favorable sex position you can have.

JACK
Talk about personal opinions. But I also get my kicks on my classic casting couch.

MARIE ANNE
Don't want hear this. Thought you hated all Hollywood ways.

JACK
But in Hollywood, the producer only goes after the innocence of young women. Here I go after the nastiness of the young man who has already taken advantage of his very young, naïve girlfriend.

I upset you do this.

JACK (getting angry)
Why---Why ? If people are dumb enough to
think they can build their relationship
into a mushroom of tender caring feelings,
then they deserve to be taken advantage of.
(almost shouting) That is all that sex is: one
explosive animalistic lust !!!!

MARIE-ANN
What about AIDS ?

JACK
I pass out condoms to anyone who comes into my
office. And anyway, we just fool around a bit----
nothing serious.

MARIE ANNE
It's his acting skills-----

JACK (angrier)
Yes, and I will give that to him. If he gives
me some sexual pleasure. Then I will make his
dreams come true. Give him some small acting
walk-on in a movie.

MARIE ANNE
It's you men. You turn into beasts.

JACK
No, it's you women who are the same. You all
hate sex.

MARIE ANNE
No, we Quebecois just put sex in its proper

place. We use it as a portal for something
richer in life.

                    JACK
How can you be rich if you don't have sex?

                 MARIE ANNE
Men search for sex to find love. Whereas women
search for love to find sex.

                    JACK
Don't tell me. I know--- ah-----.

                 MARIE ANNE
Playboy Creator? Hugh Heffner?

                    JACK
Look who's talking. He said that women were
only interested in sex.

                 MARIE ANNE
Well, maybe that's the reason you only like
younger guys.They're the only ones who can get
it up enough for you.

                    JACK
But a lot of the younger ones are too
inexperienced.

                 MARIE ANNE
Better yet, tell them you're a producer, and
they'll get it up for you.

                    JACK
Boy this is some intellectual discussion we are
having.

MARIE ANNE
It's all right if we ask personal questions at
times. We'll be working a lot of this project.

JACK
But you must have swarms of guys attacking you.

MARIE ANNE
And you know what they want.

JACK
Where is all that Montreal feminism !!

MARIE ANNE
I didn't say they would get it that easy. By
the way, are you free this Friday evening?
Something you would like at Le Garage.

JACK
Well, let me check our schedule. Our actors
don't arrive til next week, and Michel's away.
No production meeting !!

MARIE ANNE
Good. I might be able to set you up with
someone young and very athletic. And you might
like him because he is in a show.

JACK
Marie-Anne, I will take back everything I said
about you. You <u>are </u>a pimp!

MARIE ANNE
Not a nice comment to someone who is trying to
help you.

                    JACK
But are you sure he is Gay ?

                 MARIE ANNE
I knew him extremely well. Too well. But now
it's over.

                    JACK
Your ex-straight boyfriend !! No way

                 MARIE ANNE
But underneath it all, I think he really Gay.

                    JACK
You're using me as a guinea pig. You're up to
no-good, Marie-Ann.

                 MARIE ANNE
Underneath it all, maybe I do love him a lot.
But now I just want him out of my life. He's
now doing Gay porno, and I find that really
distasteful.

                    JACK
But he's only doing it for the money. He's just
showing off his precious jewels. I don't think
he's really hot for the guys.

                 MARIE ANNE
He seemed to be really into it when I saw his
first one. 19. And built like a star football
player-----and of course, a porn star.

                    JACK
Must be super attractive.

MARIE ANNE
Yes, or no. Do you want to come with me, Friday
night?

JACK
And you want me to watch him make a porno film?

MARIE ANNE
No, silly. I just think there is------
possibilities for a more serious relationship.

JACK
And to make you feel good at night that he's
really Gay. And that would be why he does not
like you that much. And you would like that?

MARIE ANNE
No, I really think he would get off having some
older guy like you steer him in the right
direction.

JACK
Just like a woman----Protection, security.
(pause) Anyway, I'll give it a shot. Why not.
And I like going to Le Garage anyway.

MARIE ANNE
Good.

JACK
But as I have told you over and over again……..
With me there are no relationships. Just lap
dances, one night stands, and escort services.

MARIE ANNE
Fine. I give up.

                    JACK
But not until we finish the most important
thing.

                  MARIE ANNE
Find out where he lives?

                    JACK
NO. Finish the budget.

(BLACKOUT)

SCENE THREE

The Scott's Living Room. Very early morning.
The sumptuous living room of Justin Scott's
prestigious house overlooking the San Francisco
Bay. Justin Scott, a handsome psychoanalyst
in his late forties, is seated at his desk,
keyboarding on his Electric typewriter, right
next to a very fashionable, large sofa. His
wife, JoAnn Scott, a very smart, attractive
woman for her middle ages, is sipping coffee
as she looks out of the foyer open window
overlooking the Bay, right in Sausalito.

                    JOANN
Does anyone get tired of just looking out at
the Golden Gate ?

                    JUSTIN (typing)
Not at this hour. That's why I insisted on this
house. Just look at that early morning sun Just
dancing around the bay. As soon as I saw the
dawn from the car, I knew I had to have it.

                    JOANN
You were right, Justin. A beautiful house,
having some of the best architecture on the
hill------

                    JUSTIN
And the most expensive in Sausalito. I'm never
satisfied with second best. Very lucrative for
a psychoanalyst like myself. People here even
want their dogs analyzed.

                    JOANN (walking over to Justin)
As usual, right on the mark.

                         JUSTIN
So why don't you live in it, and enjoy it with me.

                         JOANN
What on earth are you talking about. Make
sense, will you ?

                         JUSTIN
You spend more time in his room, then in
the bedroom with me. Some stupid surrogate
relationship--------I should get my colleague
John Talbot to take you on.

                         JOANN
For God's sake, stop all your stupid
psychoanalysis. Don't you get tired of it at
work !!

                         JUSTIN
Don't you get tired wasting all your energy in
this tremendous depression over him.

                         JOANN
I am his Mother !! Don't you think I would
spend six months worried about him? Not a word.
No phone call. No telegram. not even hearing
his beat up car driving up-----

                         JUSTIN
We put out a missing persons with the police.

                         JOAN
They have too many "run aways" to deal with.
Take a look at what downtown is becoming.

JUSTIN

Do you think we really failed that much as
parents? Look at all that whininghe would
do that when he would return home from Bay
School-----

JOANN

Justin, I can't believe you are talking like
this.

JUSTIN

Joan, I am just trying to help you. Look at all
those hours wasted in having to constantly go
over to the school to talk to the principal.
Look at all time you had to spend in helping
him with his homework, or even having to make
sure he DID his required work. You didn't have
to spend all that time with Susie. And look
where she is now. You should have gotten the
diploma, not Joey.

JOANN

Susie did not have the problems Joey had.

JUSTIN

There you go, constantly defending him again.

JOANN (abruptly)

You know Debbie, Barbara's daughter.

JUSTIN

Yes, Debbie was Joey's girl friend. I know
that. But I thought it was all over with.

JOANN

She called me. She just got a letter from Joey.

                         JUSTIN
What about it?

                         JOANN
Debbie knows he is in Canada now----Montreal

                         JUSTIN
That's great. Your hometown.

                         JOANN
I was just five years old when I left with my
Mother.

        (A slight pause.)

                         JUSTIN
I It would be great if he were enrolled in
McGill. (pause) Do you think it's true.

                         JOANN
Debbie is pretty sharp----

                         JUSTIN
I still don't think he would go all the way up
there. You did say his car was not working ok?

                         JOANN
Barbara said that a few months ago, when she
was up for the Winter Festival, that all she
smelled when entering the city was marijuana.

                         JUSTIN
Now you know he is there-----

                         JOANN
Debbie is also very concerned about Joey.

JUSTIN

I don't understand----

JOANN

The news says there are many young men in
Montreal who sell their bodies and sleep at
night in the park, selling and buying drugs.
Much has changed since I left there. And I'm
really afraid for Joey, especially with AIDS
going around.

JUSTIN

It's too cold in Montreal to do that, so get
those stupid ideas out of your mind, Joann. And
I certainly do not see my son as a gigolo for
either female or male. And definitely not for
male.

JOANN

You must be the most homophobic psychoanalyst
ever.

JUSTIN

You know that's ridiculous, and we've been
through this before. You helped me on my last
book, which made us both a lot of money.
(standing up and looking sternly at JoAnn)
My formula for happiness is adjustment to the
prevalent norms of society. Acclamation to your
environment is what makes you adjusted. Not
just yoga and meditation.

JOANN

I'm too much aware of it.

JUSTIN

There were many fine young men, even slightly

effeminate boys, whom I counseled to come
out brazenly in their workplace, with their
straight friends. There were many patients
of mine whom I counseled through their
trans-gender operation, and gave them much
support-------.

                    JOANN
I have heard this again and again, and I'm sick
of it----

 JUSTIN (sitting down again at his typewriter)
Joey is NOT transgender and certainly not
effeminate. He was a star wrestler for god's
sake. And he would have been a top scholar had
he put his mind to it---And not played around
with cocaine.

(After a slight pause, JoAnn walks up to Justin
to confront him.)

                    JOANN
I want you to go to Montreal and try to find
Joey for me. (pause) I'm very, very worried.
I can't leave my classes at Stanford now, but
you can afford to take a break. And it would be
very difficult for me to go back.

                JUSTIN (sarcastic)
I know. It is a very simple task. Montreal is
only twice the size of San Francisco.

                    JOANN
Barbara says there is someone in your
graduating class who has been living in
Montreal for the last fifteen years at least.
Hemson, Hempstead-----Whatever, is his name?

JUSTIN

Not Jack Hemming ?

JOANN

That's it. Barbara said you two were very close
at Bay School ?

JUSTIN

That's ridiculous. We haven't spoken to each
other for the last twenty-five years. We would
not recognize each other. Forget it.

JOANN

Justin, this is important. I am asking you-----

JUSTIN (yelling)

And I am telling you NO. I will not do it.
Long pause.

     (JoAnn walks over to the window. Then she
     slowly turns around and walks back to the
     desk where Justin is.)

JOANN

Justin, you remember what you were like 5 years
ago this time?

JUSTIN

You must be talking about that winter when my
Father died. I do not know why you are bringing
that up now. To see him fade away in that
hospital for four months. What a depressing
damn thing that was.

JOANN

And what did you keep telling me?

JUSTIN

It killed me to see him age so much in that
last week.

JOANN

So much that you needed me by your side. I went
out of my way to be with you. When a person you
loved so much started to fade way.

JUSTIN

Damn you. I know where you're going with this.

JOANN

My son is starting to fade away from me.
But I want him back. That is not too much for
a mother to ask. Either you go to Montreal and
make an attempt, or---or---I will have to leave
you.

(BLACKOUT)

SCENE FOUR

Le GARAGE---STOCK ROOM
What is used both as a stock room and a
dressing room for the Garage Bar. Cardboard
crates of Beer, Whisky, and Vodka line up some
of the back wall. A few old tables and chairs
sit around the backstage, where the strippers
can talk and network with some of their
clients.
Bill and Donny rush in laughing, this time
wearing bikini bathing suits.

                    BILL
She pinched my ass, that bitch. See the
expression on her face.

                    DONNY
But check this out, that blond. Now she fuckin'
knows how to kiss.

(Both continue to laugh among themselves.)

                    BILL
Many were hot for you, man.

                    DONNY
See how scared they were when I started
lowering my trunks. Hell, It's wild up here.
You can show them your cock, butt, your nuts,
and all.They could touch anything, if they
wanted.

                    BILL
As a first timer, you knocked them dead. But you
gotta keep it back for women.

(After a pause.)

                    DONNY
Your girl friend. Whatta she think?

                    BILL
I think she's ok. Especially when you held
back. She's like that. I'm setting you up, man.

    (They do a hug among themselves.)

                    DONNY
You sure you okay with this? Gotta another
bitch on the side ?

                    BILL
I know what I want. And I can get it.

        (At this moment, Marie Anne timidly enters
        from Stage Right, along with Jack)

                    MARIE ANN
You guys decent?

                    DONNY
Ah----(throws his hand over his crotch, and
very affected) This is so embarrassing !!

                    MARIE ANNE
You too foolish. Bathing suits you got on.

            BILL (goes to kiss her)
I know you hate this. But I'm glad you came to
our show anyway.

                    MARIE ANNE
Just wanna make sure you get food on the table.

                              BILL
You gotta do what you hate doing at times.

                          MARIE ANNE
Tell me about it ----- like spending hours
working on budgets for movies.

                              BILL
But Andre doesn't do girls right. He knows some
of them do not bring in good money.

Jack slowly walks in behind Judy.

                          MARIE ANNE
This is Jack Hemming, the Producer I intern
under.

                              BILL
Sorry about this being a sleazy place.

                              JACK
I used to come here quite a bit. But now that I
see you, I should come here more often. But you
do look familiar.

                          MARIE ANNE
Je le regrette. C'est Bill Mitchell et son ami
----- ah

                              BILL
Donny Nickelson !!!

                          MARIE ANNE
Like you, they are Americans.

          BILL (extends his hand to Jack)

Forgive my lousy French. Marie Anne knows that

                    JACK
That's all right. As I said, I have been here a
number of times. I'm not going to hide it.

                    BILL
Come here another night, and I will give you a
dance.

                    JACK
Now I remember. You've already given me a
couple. Your lap dances are the best. The very
best--- tres bien.

                    BILL
You probably got me mixed up with someone else.
I never forget a person I have danced with.

                    JACK
There's always the first time,

                    BILL
Sorry about that, man. (starts to come on to
him) But you look----Good.

                    JACK
Not important. But, as I said. I like what I
see. (takes out his card) Can I----you know----
can I---take you out after your
Shift is over. A private show?

                    BILL
Super !!

                    JACK
Not tonight. Perhaps another night ?

BILL
Sure. But I don't come cheap.

JACK
I would hope not. But you have a very familiar
look.

BILL
Hey, let's do it. (walks back to Donny) I'm
sorry. I neglected Donny. (to everyone) Donny
Nickelson. Newly arrived from the States---from
California.

MARIE ANNE
Bien Venue

DONNY
Welcome? Right? I'm trying to learn. I'm even
trying
to make friends. But my French is so bad, and
no one wants
to know a dumb American.

MARIE ANNE
You're doing ok.

DONNY
You're not so bad yourself. (pause) I mean-
----I mean you're really hot-------I mean
beautiful.

        (Donny continues starring at Marie-Anne)

JACK
Where you say you were from again?

        (Donny breaks from his trance.)

                    DONNY
I'm sorry. (pause) Oh---ah----San Francisco
----California

                    JACK
Beautiful city.

                    DONNY
Used to be.

                    JACK
I grew up there.

                    DONNY
Where?

                    JACK
Near Sausalito.

                    DONNY
Awesome !!! Hey, they said you were a producer?

                    JACK
Right there----

                    DONNY
Bill and I just made a short film. Here—The VHS
cover photos

        (Donny takes out the card board cover.)

                    DONNY
Now it should be in the video stores.

                    BILL
Donny !!

JACK

No problem. I'd like to see a few minutes.

    (Donny holds up his cardboard photos. THE
    GROUP AT FIRST BECOME GLUED TO WHAT THEY
    SEE, not knowing at first what it is.)

JACK

Porno ? Good.

DONNY

Damn you, Bill. They do more close ups of you.
Where are mine?

BILL (sarcastic)

Right. I'll tell Miguel to change the cover.

MARIE ANNE (becoming impatient)

I'm leaving everybody. You can do your own
thing without me.

    (Marie Anne starts to leave. Donny puts
    down the cardboard cover and runs in front
    of Judy.)

DONNY

I'm sorry. Miss Cadieux. Please, I've thrown
the pictures away. See. Please. I ain't gonna
do it again. Promise. I won't do it again. Just
like tonight. I just needed the money.

BILL

Marie Anne is a "French" Puritan.

DONNY

No, I'm sorry. Please, you seem to be a very
respectable lady. I won't do it again. Please,

I really would like to see you again. Maybe
you---you know - maybe------

                    MARIE ANNE
Yes, Donny. What it it? Say it?

                    DONNY
My French is very bad, and I ain't got many
friends up here. (pause) Maybe you could
introduce me. To some people to get—you know---
a decent job.

                    MARIE ANNE
Just no more "sexual" animation.

                    DONNY
Let me walk you out.

                    MARIE ANNE
Well, if you get your clothes on quickly, I
make take you up on it. I just don't go out
with nude men.

        (Donny rushes to get his clothes.)

                    DONNY
I'll call you in a few, Bill.

        (Donny rushes to the back to get his
        pants, then exits with July.)

                    BILL
We're all alone. Now we can really party.

                    JACK
You have a face that's quite astonishing.
Beautiful look - beautiful body. But, I usually

cannot afford to get caught up with feelings like this.

                    BILL
So don't knock it, man. Remember my shit full of happiness? Don't tell me you forgot my lap dance?

                    JACK
Ah, don't give me that baloney.

                    BILL
But it's true. I thought you were someone special.

                    JACK
(stares intently) But it's your face.

                    BILL
Yeah.

                    JACK
I think I've known it from the past. I do not know why. (pause) Maybe it's that lap dance that you claim you don't remember.

                    BILL
Maybe you need someone older

                    JACK
No, I'm really into younger guys-----And I got the money.
And that's all that matters when I date.

                    BILL
Yeah, I dig you. I can get into older guys. And now I'm starting to remember that lap dance.

                    JACK
I never thought my age would help me that much.

                    BILL
And might be interested in more than just a
show.

                    JACK
Good.

                    BILL
J'ai ceci. Mecredi, Mardy, Vendredi, Samedi

            JACK (touches his face)
I will be back then.

                    BILL
As I said, I am open to a lot of things.

        (Jack and Bill gently kiss each on the
        neck, French style.)

        (Then Jack exits.)

Bill rubs his hair in wonder, then snaps to it
and goes upstage to put on his pants.

(BLACKOUT)

SCENE FIVE

HOTEL QUEEN ELIZABETH --- MONTREAL. The interior of an upscale hotel room at The Elizabeth. Doors lead to a back bedroom, with various antique designed furniture spaced throughout the room. Justin is sitting onstage right, talking on his hotel phone. It is cordless, so he can move around.

> JUSTIN (to the person on the other end)
> Yes----yes......I talked with him, and he is due to arrive at my hotel room anytime now---------Of course, I would not go to a cheap dive-------I do not know------Yes, Yes----.I will hunt out Miles End. I know, where you grew up------------------- But I will call later tonight.

Justin then hangs up. He then takes out his portable tape recorder to begin recording. Suddenly the phone rings from downstairs.

> JUSTIN
> ....Yes, let him up.

Justin then closes his notebook. He does some last minute straightening up of the room. Then there is a knock on the door. Justin opens it.

> JUSTIN
> Jack Hemming. (pauses) I have not seen you for years.

> JACK
> Dr. Scott, I presume. I never thought you were that into books.

GAY FOR PAY   40

                    JUSTIN
You've kept yourself well.

                    JACK
Bien Venue au Montreal.

                    JUSTIN
Don't just stand there. Come in.

Jack enters the hotel room, a little more
dressy than he was when he was at Le Garage.
There is an awkward pause.

                    JUSTIN
Sit down.

                    JACK
After all these years, I could not believe it
was your voice on the phone. (pause) I hate to
say it, but you still look good, Justin. I'll
never forget those wrestling matches of yours.

                    JUSTIN
If we randomly met each other on the streets,
do you think we would recognize each other.

            JACK (slightly angry)
No. We would fight it out between us.

                    JUSTIN
That bad, huh.

            JACK (louder)
Don't you remember, How at the end. How much we
hated each other. We're lucky we're talking.

JUSTIN (clearing his throat)
Anyway, thanks so much for coming here. I'm
really sorry for not writing you back. And I
can't blame you for being angry, especially
because of what happened.

JACK (more intensity)
Did my letters sound angry. Or do you remember?

JUSTIN (embarrassed)
My memory. I'm sorry.

JACK
You forget. I did NOT get my diploma. But-----
I was not going to college, and I did not need
a recommendation.

(Justin is taken back)

JUSTIN
I do remember. I'm sorry. I must have left you
quite broken hearted.

JACK
Don't regret it. I never allow myself to get
involved emotionally.

JUSTIN
But your letters.

JACK
Wild ideas, wild aspirations. I was just a
crazy kid then. (pause) But what it you so
urgently wanted to see me about. I scarcely
think you would want to invest in one of my
movies?How did you know I was here?

                    JUSTIN
Remember Barbara-------Oh, I'm sorry. Sit down.

        (They both sit opposite each other.)

                    JACK
I very casually wrote her a short letter a few
months ago. I do not know why I did it.

                    JUSTIN
She is now editor of the Alumni Review. You
tell her what you are having for dinner that
night, and all of Bay School alumni will know
the next morning.

                    JACK
I hope that's not all she knows about me

                    JUSTIN
We know the real important thing. A Canadian
film producer. What an accomplishment. And a six
figure salary-----

                    JACK
That's all Americans think about. How much
money each other makes-----

                    JUSTIN
Why not? Nothing else matters------

                    JACK
Other things matter to you. All that time you
spent on your very successful book Barbara told
me about that?

                    JUSTIN
I only did it to boost my practice. More

books sold would only make more patients. More patients, bigger return. And as I said in my acknowledgement, I really thank my wife for helping me get it together. Without her, I wouldn't have been able to do it.

                    JACK
But the excitement of coming up with new psychological theories------

                    JUSTIN
There you go. You still haven't grown up. Still mesmerized by all your stupid idealistic ideas. You haven't changed.

                    JACK
Well, I hope everyone in stupid Bay School knows that now I'm an "out" Gay man. All my staff at the studio know.

(An awkward pause.)

                    JUSTIN
That's not important----

                    JACK
You're still evading the Gay issue------

                    JUSTIN (standing up)
I'm not evading it. It was never there !! You're still holding a grudge.

                    JACK
Not really. I have forgotten all about it.

                    JUSTIN
I'm sorry, Jack. Please, please try to forgive me----

                              JACK
No hard feelings. In fact, there are few soft
feelings in my life now. Ever since I came out,
I just hunt down boys, strip clubs or indulge
myself in paying for one-night stands. I really
don't believe in relationships.

                             JUSTIN
Then forget the disciplinary situation, Jack.
Don't let it hang onto you like this

                         JACK (angrier)
Not for me. It was the principle behind the
situation, and I'll be damned if I was in the
wrong. Be honest, Justin, you must still hate
my guts. And for the life of me, I don't know
why you came all the way to Montreal just to
see me----

(Slight pause.)
                             JUSTIN
I did not come up here just for old times sake.

                              JACK
Then what is it ?

                             JUSTIN
I came up to Montreal to find my son. …. (pause)
And please…… (pause)
Please….. you're the only one who can help me
! ! !

    (BLACK OUT)

ACT TWO

SCENE ONE

Hotel QUEEN Elizabeth. Jack and Justin are situated in very much the same situation they were a few minutes ago, again in a very upscale room at the Hotel Queen Elizabeth. The scene picks up where we left off.

JACK

Why me? Is he Gay ?

JUSTIN (angry)

Of course not. Why you say that ?

JACK

There you go again. If you continue with this hostility, I will not help you.

JUSTIN

I mean------I don't know. Maybe----maybe not !! The point is-------He ran away from home.

JACK

How old is he?

JUSTIN

Nineteen.

JACK

Kind of old for running away-----maybe he's just trying to find himself. Do you have a picture

JUSTIN

Yes, but it's in my suitcase. I will have to get if for you. (pause) But it's my wife. She is desperately worried. We haven't heard from him for the last six months. No phone calls, no letters,

                    JACK
Missing persons ?

                    JUSTIN
No luck. I even hired a detective who "thinks" he ran away to Canada. Joey 's driver's license it still missing. And he has been writing hisex-girl friend a few times. And she told us he was here.

                    JACK
Well—let's see what we can do. All I can do is take you to all the clubs.I'll even take you to Park Champlain. But as you know I am a very, very busy man. Justin, you have to pay me much for this.

                    JUSTIN
You know I can pay you a lot. (pause) Jack, it's my wife. I have to find him. I can't go back without some contact information. And my wife's leaving would really devastate me.

                    JACK
Now I can see why you never answered my letters. Do you still live in California?

                    JUSTIN
Yes. My wife and I live just north of San Francisco. Sausalito.

(Jack then gets out of his chair. He pauses for a few minutes, as he paces around the room.)

                    JACK

I'm just trying to remember. This current kid I
know has an American friend-----

                    JUSTIN

Where is he from?

                    JACK

San Francisco. And he's also into sports---
wrestling, probably football. Good looking kid.
About 20 or so. And I think he's been here less
than------two months?

            JUSTIN (highly exuberant)

I bet that's him. It's gotta be him. Christ, I
can't believe this. This is unbelievable luck.

                    JACK

I will contact you. Give me a few days. I might
be able to get him up here. He's a very good
friend of this American male dancer/hustler
that I'm paying.

                    JUSTIN

I owe you----

                    JACK

Forget it. My anger a few minutes ago got the
best of me.

                    JUSTIN

But you don't know how much relief you have
given me.

                    JACK

Keep in mind, we don't for sure if he is the
one-----

                    JUSTIN
But you are trying to help me, after all that
we have gone through.

An important pause here.

                    JACK
Justin-----Justin. One important thing. (pause)
Why did you go into psychology?
Become an analyst ? You were never in it
before.

                    JUSTIN
A steak, champagne dinner for both us, if this
kid
Is my son. There we will talk.

                    JACK
Yes, we have to talk.

(BLACKOUT)

SCENE TWO

INSIDE JACK HEMMING'S VILLAGE APARTMENT. It
is morning. Both Bill and Jack have had sex
together. Now Jack relaxes, while smoking.
Both are lying in bed. Bill then rouses himself
off the bed. He stands up, while rubbing his ass.

                    BILL
You're a tough guy in bed, man.

                    JACK
Coming from a porn star, that must be a
compliment.

Bill walks over to his back pack, pulls out a
VHS cassette and hands it to Jack.

                    BILL
I brought the porno. You said you wanted to
borrow it. I've got an extra cassette.

                    JACK
Thanks. I will certainly enjoy looking at it.
But I think I can show it to someone who can
get you a larger acting job In the movies.

                    BILL
You're the producer. But I still think they
should have done more close ups of Donny.

                    JACK
But you still get a good look at his body.
Everyone will know it is him. Anyway, that's
not your problem.

BILL

He's a fresh kid. He's new to everything in
Montreal. I don't want him to get into any
trouble.

JACK

So, what are you going to do for the rest of
your life. Keep modeling, dancing-----making
money in the sex trade.

BILL

I love doing this work. What's wrong with
it, and the money is really GOOD. You're now
sounding like my old man. But a "Good ole man."
One I never had.

JACK

Don't worry. I'm not a prude. But you're not
going to be a "sexy hot stud" forever. As you
get older, you'll have to find something else.

(Bill walks towards the window.)

BILL

Whatever I do in life, it has to be my own thing.
I just can't----I really can't work for someone
else. That's real prostitution---Not this.

JACK

We all have to face that brick wall someday.
Why did you leave the States?

BILL

I just couldn't stand it at home. Too many stop
signs. My mom, ok. My old man, I couldn't take
anymore. So one night, I snuck out of the house,
withdrew all my money from my savings account.

                    JACK
That's taking a risk.

                    BILL
I bought a Greyhound bus ticket that would take
me as far away as possible. I did not care how
long or how far the bus would carry me.Just set
me somewhere totally different from where I was.
After about twenty hours on the road, I was
told to get out. That was as far as the ticket
would get me.

                    JACK
Montreal ?

                    BILL
No----St. Louis ---with only four dollars in
my wallet. I wondered about the city. I didn't
know what I was going to do. I really didn't
care. It was a bit on the chilly side, so I
realized I had to get some shelter.

                    JACK
Makes sense-----

                    BILL
I came to the high steps of this large church.
It was very late at night, so it was closed.
No one was around, so I figured I could bed
down. I slept for I don't know how long. Then
I heard someone coming slowly up the church
steps. I said to myself. This could be it.
Maybe the cops, or maybe some fuck-ass that
was going to try to mug me. I pretended to
still be asleep. Then the steps stopped. I
then felt a little bit of a breeze hover over
me. The steps went away. About ten minutes

later, I got up. I then saw to my amazement what the breeze was. Two one hundred dollar bills were laid at my feet. God had blessed me like never before. I could do whatever I wanted with them.

JACK

So you came to Montreal.

BILL

I came to a city where Jesus looked over us from the top of a mountain.

(Jack walks over and gives more money to Bill.)

JACK

This is against my grain. But could I see you for one more time. I'll pay you. But I think I am actually starting to have some feeling for you.

BILL (thumbs up)

All for broke, man. But the feeling. I don't know about that.

JACK

But this time I will give you a hotel room at the Queen Elizabeth thatI will be staying at. And you must bring Donny.

BILL

Now this is starting to sound weird

JACK

No, it isn't. This director who works under me will most likely want to cast you both in a

major feature---<u>non</u>-porno. Here, let me give
you this address.

    (Jack walks out of bed and goes over to
    his small desk counter. He writes on a
    small sheet of paper.)

                  BILL
I don't believe this.

                  JACK
Believe it. This is the hotel room you should
be at tomorrow afternoon at that time.

                  BILL
Hotel Elizabeth?

                  JACK
Only the best. But you must also bring Donny.

                  BILL
This is like a dream. But we'll be there.
If we have to put out, we'll do that.

    (Bill folds up the note and starts to walk
    out. Then he turns around and walks back
    to Jack to hug him.)

                  BILL
Like I said, I now remember. You were my best
lap dance.

    (Bill then leaves.)

(BLACKOUT)

SCENE THREE

The small apartment of Marie Anne Cadieux,
located in Miles End, northern Montreal.
There is darkness at first. Then screams by
Marie Anne.
In the very dim light we see her jumping out of
bed and hurrying to the bathroom.)
Danny rises from the bed and turns on the
light. He picks up a cigarette, then gets up
and walks around. He is in his jockey shorts.
He hears some noise from the bathroom.

                    DONNY
Marie Anne-----Marie Anne

                    MARIE ANNE
Leave me alone.

                    DONNY
Look, I'm sorry. Damn it. I really am.

                    MARIE ANNE
Pis de. Calisse de mon appartement !!

          (Donny takes a beat, then turns back to
          the door.)

                    DONNY
I'm not going to leave you like this.

                    MARIE ANNE
Yeah, right. After you get off rocks, you
apologize. Just leave. (crying)

                    DONNY
Please-please Marie Ann. Come out so I can make

it up to you. I don't have nobody in the city.
Please---please---

>   (There is another pause, then slowly the
>   door opens. Marie Anne steps onto the
>   stage, as they are both alone in the
>   room.)

MARIE ANNE

Everyman I meet? Every single man I meet. The
first thing they want is get off. Get off. That's
all they care about.

DONNY

Come on----Don't be so angry.

MARIE ANNE

You know what I'm sayin' You know damn well
what I'm sayin' It's all same with men. They
want to dazzle everyone with sex. But women
want a kind, sincere man. Sex can be gentle and
compassionate, and honest. What's wrong with
that !!

DONNY

You should have told me you didn't want it back
there. Sweetheart, you got a nice piece there.
And I'm a young horny bull. Hey, Billy, your
ex-- he really got into it.

>   (Marie Anne starts to walk around the
>   bedroom.)

MARIE ANNE

Everyone's different. You got to meet the person
where he is.

                    DONNY

Well, I'm here.

                  MARIE ANNE

So whatta you here for? I thought I met a
gentleman the other night----Someone special. A
guy who can do things other than sex. (pause)
So whatta do? You want to go out for movies,
plays? Read books ? You must be interested in
things other than hockey games?

                    DONNY

You're on, Mari Anne. We'll go to a movie
together.

                  MARIE ANNE

We'll go to a great French film. Don't forget,
I'm a Quebecois film-maker.

                    DONNY

But I won't understand it unless they speak
English.

                  MARIE ANNE

All right. So what kind of music you like?
There must be something you like to dance to?

        (Donny starts to pace around the room.)

                    DONNY

Just like my stupid mother----always poking her
nose intomy business. That's why I ran away.

                  MARIE ANNE

Don't get so macho on me. Just trying to help
us cometogether other than sex.

DONNY

All right. Do you like "The Boss"?

MARE ANNE

Qui est "The Boss" ?

DONNY

All right, forget it. I'll go to a French film
with you, and then we'll go to an American
action film.

MARIE ANNE.

Sound stupid. But ok.

DONNY

Then we'll have sex your way?

MARIE ANNE

Donny, when I agreed to go out with you, I told
youI wanted it to be something more than just
sex.

DONNY

But I gotta get it off with someone. I just
can't whack off every night.

MARIE ANN

Whack off?

DONNY

Forget it !!!

MARIE ANNE

But Donny. Your life. I find you very
intriguing. And I want to help you. You no do
sex games the rest of your life.

                    DONNY

But as I told you, I gotta make the money. I
can't return to the States. My father would
kill me for running away, and send me to some
Technical School, or insist I join the army
or something.

                    MARIE ANNE

But let me get to really know you---as
someone other thana body in bed. Our love
making then would be mature.

                    DONNY

Maybe if I did straight porn, you would be
able to love better.

     (Marie-Ann stands up.)

                    MARIE ANNE

No-no. We go to the Federal Office here in
Montreal to get you a Work Visa, so you can
stay here longer and get a career job.

                    DONNY

So I will have more time to make love your
way, and meet more English speaking people?

                    MARIE ANNE

Why not?

                    DONNY

But that's why I ran away from my "ole man."
I didn't want to learn how to become ---you
know—An electrician. I want to do something
more Interesting.

MARIE-ANN

Doing a lot of stupid sex acts in front of camera. That interesting?

DONNY

But it's the money !!

MARIE ANNE

Electricians make very good money. It's a good job. Bien

DONNY

Be--- what?

MARIE ANNE

Je le mets en place, et tu travailles avec moi.

DONNY

In English----English

MARIE ANNE

We work out something. Didn't you tell me you wanted to live better than on Frontenac. You won't be able to unless you make decent money on a decent job .

DONNY

But I also want you.

MARIE ANNE

No, you don't. You see me just as an object. Some ass you can fuck anytime you want.

DONNY

But I do care for you. Why are you giving me such a hard time.

                        MARIE ANNE
We Montreal women are coming into our own. Just
like the Gays coming out and do fun in public.

                          DONNY
But I am not Gay.

                  MARIE ANNE (sarcastic)
Yes, I know. You just have sex with them in
front of the camera.

                          DONNY
But I just do it for the money. And I want to
make enough money so we can both be happy.

        (There is a pause here.)

                        MARIE ANNE
So you can stay more in Miles End with me. Then
you can enroll at Aviron, a very good technical
school---

                          DONNY
Ain't interested----

                        MARIE ANNE
Je le mets en place, et tu travailles avec moi.
And anyway, Le Garage is "closing."

                          DONNY
Yeah, but Bill called me today. Opening new Gay
clubs at St. Cathereeine, I guess. But I don't
know people there.

                        MARIE ANNE
All right. I can get Jack to get you a job
there.

                    DONNY
Super.

                    MARIE ANNE
But you got to go to Aviron first.

(There is a pause.)

                    DONNY
But I can live with you in Miles End?

                    MARIE ANN
Yes. But you also go to Aviron.

                    DONNY
O.K. It's a deal.

                    MARIE ANN
Deal?

                    DONNY
But one more thing.

                    MARIE ANNE
I don't think I want to hear this.

                    DONNY
Just let me make one more porno. My last one.

                    MARIE ANNE
We will talk.

        (Marie Anne walks back to the bathroom
        door.)

(BLACKOUT)

SCENE FOUR

INSIDE THE HOTEL ELIZABETH
Justin is in his hotel suite, writing in his
notebook. Suddenly the downstairs phone rings,
and he stands up to answer it.

JUSTIN
Yes......tell him to come up.

After Justin puts the phone down, he goes over
to close up the tape machine. Then he paces
around the room nervously. There is a knock at
the door, and Justin goes to open it. It is
Jack Hemming.

JUSTIN
Thanks so much for your news.

JACK
I think it is him.

JUSTIN (nervously)
Are you absolutely sure? Did he answer up
to his identity? Was he angry?

JACK
I couldn't start a conversation with him about
it. Else he wouldn't come up here.

JUSTIN
You invited him here.? Why not a public place.
A bar or a restaurant?

JACK
Why not here? You seem to be afraid that he
would get violent or something.

                    JUSTIN
He ran off perhaps to get away from us. I tried
telling JoAnn that.

                    JACK
Sit down for a minute. I have something to
show you. He and my friend won't be here for a
while.

                    JUSTIN
Jack, you are playing games again.

        (Jack takes out the cassette and places
        it in the video recorder in the hotel
        room, so Justin can clearly see the porno
        video.)

                    JACK
I want you to look at this video.

                    JUSTIN
What is this? Something you produced?

                    JACK
No. Definitely not.

        (The video starts to play. The audience
        can not see what is on the TV screen.)

                JUSTIN (laughing)
What is this? A stupid porno film?

                    JACK
Look again.

        (Justin looks at the video wide-eyed. Then
        the grimace turns to dismay. He is silent

for a few minutes before he begins to speak. Justin gets up, and very angrily starts to walk to the other side of the room. He addresses Jack.)

JUSTIN (with intensity)
Why did you show that to me? You made my son have sex in front of the camera just to be in one ofyour low grade films?

JACK
No. Just to show you what your son is doing.

(Justin continues to pace.)

JUSTIN
I think it was childish for you to show me that video----

JACK
I was just trying to show you what he is getting into here in Montreal.

JUSTIN (angrier)
No you weren't. You were just trying to prove that I was a failure as a father, that I can't even psychoanalyze my own son. So it's a porno? So what? Nowadays it's legal.

JACK
I was just trying to prove to you that he does have a little bit of a Gay streak.

JUSTIN
No. You were trying to get even with me, after all these years.

(Suddenly the downstairs phone rings
again. Justin slowly goes to answer it.)

JUSTIN

Who----What--------(PAUSE) All right just let
them up.

(Justin turns to Jack.)

JUSTIN

You told them to come now. Damn it. Are you
tryingto trick me again?

JACK

But I had to get them all up here in order to
get your son Donny up here.

JUSTIN

His name is Joey. God, I hope you have the
right one.

JACK

That's just the name he goes by up here.

(The door bell buzzes. Justin goes to
answer it. He opens the door and both Bill
and Donny walk in.)

BILL

Hey, Jack. What a layout here. You say this
producer-----

(Suddenly Billy stops in his tracks when
he sees who is in the room.)

BILL

DAD. What the fuckin' hell is this?

                         JUSTIN
Joey, I had to come to Montreal to find
you-----

        (Jack is shocked when he hears this.)

                          JACK
Where's Donny? This can't be your son.

                         DONNY
Someone call my name?

        (Bill (Joey) takes out the $100 dollar
        bills and throw them at Jack.)

                     BILL (angry)
You tricked me you fucker. I will never,
never, allow you to touch my body again. I
don't care what you have to offer me----money
or role, or what !!!

        (Justin explodes with rage when he sees
        this.)

                         JUSTIN
How dare you treat my son as a common
hustler!!

        (AT THIS MOMENT JUSTIN ATTACKS JACK AND
        PUNCHES HIM IN THE JAW !!!)

                    JACK (shouting)
I never came on you first. You damn well know
that.

        (Billy and Donny rush at Justin to pull
        him away. The fighting becomes very

intense. However, the boys' youthful
masculinity overpowers Justin's attack.
They manage to put him down.)

                BILL AND DONNY (yelling)
You're crazy man. Let him go. You wanna go to
jail.

          (As soon as they subdue Justin, there is
          a moment of intense silence. A PREGNANT
          PAUSE. Jack rubs some blood off his jaw.)

                        DONNY
I'm gettin' out of here, man, before security
or the police arrive.

                JACK (pointing to Donny)
I thought he was your son. He comes from San
Francisco.

                JUSTIN (holding his breath)
So does Joey. And his name is NOT Bill. You
should know San Francisco is a large enough
city for a guy to get lost in.

                        JACK
But the video. You saw him in the video.

                        JUSTIN
Yes, I did, you idiot. Along with this other
guy.

                JACK (to Joey)
You told me you were from the Midwest.

                    JOEY (Bill)
But I was in San Francisco before that. I
didn't want no one to know.

        (Jack looks at Joey and then at Justin.)

                    JACK
Jesus !!

                    DONNY
I'm leavin' You zulou creeps can fight it out on
your own.

                    JOEY (Bill)
I'm leavin' with you.

                    JUSTIN
Please—please, please Joey. Let me talk with
you, please. Your Mother, Joey. She's worried
sick about you.

                    JOEY
NO !!

                    JUSTIN
Please, Joey. You're my only son !!

                    JOEY
But you're not my father. Never, never the
father that I wanted.

                    JUSTIN
But why---why can't we talk about it. We have
to.

                    JOEY
Yes, now that I'm absent, you realize what a
stupid jerk You were.

JUSTIN

Why—why aren't you man enough to tell me what
I did wrong? Aren't you man enough to see how
wrong you were?

DONNY (impatient)

Bill---or whatever the hell your name is ---
Joey. I'll see you outside, man. This is the
craziest shit I've ever seen.

JACK

We should all go. This is father and son
business.

JUSTIN

No—wait---wait. Goddamn it, all of you
(catching his breath) Let me talk with Jack. I
have to apologize to him. But we need to speak
in private. But Joey, please, please, come back
in ten minutes. We all have to speak together
then.

JOEY

All right, ten-----But you twirpts gotta be
finished by then.Let's go, Donny.

DONNY

Man, that's the best thing I heard tonight.

        (Joey and Donny leave. Jack sits down
        again at the desk. Justin walks among the
        hotel room, too nervous to sit.)

JUSTIN

I know why you set this up with the video. But
you screwed my own son behind my back. You
could've made him HIV.

                    JACK
Justin, I told you I didn't know he was your
son. I thought Donny was. But don't you see.
That's not the point.

                    JUSTIN
We have to talk everything out in the open.

                    JACK
You fuckin' psychiatrist---or counselor---or
whatever the hell you are.

     (Jack then sits down, followed by Justin.)

                    JACK
You never answered my question, Justin.

                    JUSTIN
Which is ?

                    JACK
Why did you decide to become a psychoanalyst?

     (There is a pause)

                    JUSTIN
Every psychoanalyst has an answer to that.
Moments of Intense sensation that we
experienced many years ago never leave our
brain. We try to suppress them or even forget
them. They always stick with us. As analysts we
pry into those "forgotten moments."

                    JACK
I put so much feeling back in those love
letters I sent you. And you had those letters
sent back, claiming that you were not at

that address. But I knew you were. And your rejection made the hurt worse.

(Justin now gets very close to Jack. There is a brief pause.)

JUSTIN
Damn you. Don't you see, Jack. Back then peoples' attitudes towards sex were much different. Social norms are changing now, and things are beginning now to open up. Back then I could not allow myself to be involved in a relationship like that. My parents did not have that much money, and I had to get a scholarship in order to get into a good college.

JACK
Then why did you come on to me? Why did you keep telling me this was an exciting moment, that we both loved each other respectfully so much?

(Justin then stands up and walks a few paces away from Jack.)

JUSTIN
Like all kids we only thought of that immediate moment, not its repercussions. When the principal called me into his office, I had to confess to everything. If I did not cooperate with him, I would have been expelled, with a horrible note on my record that would have made it impossible for me to enter Stanford, or any other good school. My dream college and my career hinged on doing well at that stupid prep school we were at.

(Jack then stands up.)

JACK

Justin, have you ever been madly in love with
someone?

JUSTIN

Have you? You told me you never involved
yourself In feelings.

(Jack starts slowly walking up to Justin.
A slight pause.)

JACK

Except for you. And I was back then. I was
crazy about you, just as I know you were crazy
about me

JUSTIN

No----

JACK

I knew that as soon as your firm body touched
mine-----

JUSTIN

That's only because you came onto me. Pressed
it so hard on me.

JACK

There you go again with your goddamn lies. Even
today you don't have the guts to admit it. All
you care about is your rotten image to your
psychiatric colleagues and to your silly affluent
neighbors.

JUSTIN

Just like the lies you tell the "want to be
a star" young men, when you let them worship
you, adore you----

JACK

But I give them something. I give them a
chance to be in front of the camera, even if
it's just for a few minutes. You pretended to
give me your body, but what you really did is
to steal something from me. You stole away my
feelings.

        (Jack moves over to pick up his light
        jacket, in order to leave. He walks to
        the door to leave, only to be interrupted
        by Justin.)

JUSTIN

You're right, Jack. Over the years I have come
to realize how very selfish I was. I'm sorry.
Can't you accept that. I really am sorry.
Can't you forgive me? I'm sorry—sorry I lied
about your raping me.

        (Jack opens the door to leave.)

JACK

Good-bye Justin----

        (There is an awkward pause.)

JUSTIN

Please talk to me, Jack-----

        (Another pause)

                         JACK
But you DID tell me what I wanted to know. Now
I know you really loved me. That is all I
wanted to know.

                        JUSTIN
Jack, if you want to have a relationship with
my son, that is fine……..is fine------With me.

                         JACK
Let me think about it. (a long pause) Good-bye.

          (Jack leaves and shuts the door. Justin
          walks over to the other side of the room.
          After a lengthy pause, there is a knock at
          the door. Justin goes to answer it. Joey
          is back.)

                         JOEY
Now you have your ten minutes.

          (Justin and Billy (Joey) are now alone.
          They both pace around the hotel room
          alone, not looking at each other
          After a lengthy pause, Joey decides to
          break the ice, and sits down. He now looks
          directly at Justin)

                         JOEY
It was Debbie, wasn't it. I could smack the
little gossip.

                        JUSTIN
It was more your Mother putting all the pieces
together. You really hurt her. She's going for
therapy.

                    JOEY

For that, and only that, I am truly sorry. I
will not apologize for anything else. I'll say
that.

                    JUSTIN

I'll say this. I admire your perseverance for
getting into Canada.

                    JOEY

Thanks a million, Dad. Hell, you can't
complain. You inspired me.

                    JUSTIN

I wish your brain was just as good.

                    JOEY

You mean, you wished my brain agreed with
everything you say. Now I know your little Gay
secret.

                    JUSTIN

You're right. You are absolutely right. Your
little video stunt made me realize I hadn't
forgotten it.

                    JOEY

Hey---ah---- I guess. I guess. You must have
really loved him a lot.

                    JUSTIN

Yes. I guess we really did love each other
then. Yet I tried to run away from it. But I
don't wish you to run away from yours.

                    JOEY

Even though I like Jack as a friend, I only did

it for the money. I only did it for the part he was going to give me.

                    JUSTIN
Just make sure he gives you a good one---- I mean the acting part.

                    JOEY
This might sound silly, ole man------and don't give me hell for this. But sometimes------- sometimes I don't really know what I want to do.

        (Justin gets up and walks a few paces
        around the hotel room.)

                    JOEY
What about Jack? You gonna tell Mother about Him?

                    JUSTIN
It was a romance----or could have been a romance---Only to a certain degree.

                    JOEY
Whatta ya mean ?

                    JUSTIN
Maybe back then I got too caught up with my dreams---My career meant everything to me. But you have to understand. Things were very different then. Society, norms, religious beliefs---- they kind of defined us then-- -Maybe too much so. And I have just been thinking------
        (He looks squarely at Joey).
I think I am kinda proud you took off-----

                    JOEY

Don't read you now Dad.

          (Justin turns around and walks towards
          Joey's money left on the floor and picks
          it up.)

                    JUSTIN

A lot of us have become Gay for Pay. I
certainly hope you have a chance to do
better.
          (looking at Joey again)
Do you like Jack that much ?

                    JOEY

I don't know. I wouldn't have minded that
part in the film. Are you gonna tell Mother
about what you did with him-----or about my
porno film?

                    JUSTIN

No, I'm not going to tell her. Not that she
would really care. She just wants to have
living proof that you're all right. She's
very, very depressed over your absence. I
wish you could see her at the home. Your
presence would give her a smile that I have
not see on her for almost a year now.

                    JOEY

What about Jack?

          (A pause. Justin picks up his drink and
          walks to the window)

                    JUSTIN

You know, I really love your Mother-----or I

have grown to love her. Jack and I were too young to really grow into something else.

                    JOEY
You make it sound so dull.

                    JUSTIN
It's not. It just goes through changes.
(pauses) Relationships are funny things. Like walking through a dream we have absolutely no control over. But then, eventually, we---we just have to make it real. Sometimes we just have to resurrect those buried feelings and undo those illusions we have of each other. I wish I had told my patients that.

                    JOEY
It's not too late.

        (Justin walks over to get another drink)

                    JUSTIN
True, the excitement only lasts for a short amount of time. But then a new adventure opens. And hopefully both partners are open to that new adventure. And they're NOT for pay. (pause) And we really want you to be a part of that.

                    JOEY
I'm sorry. I'm really sorry.

                    JUSTIN
No. You don't have to tell me that again. But you probably will not believe this. I almost do not believe it now myself. But -----all that your Mother, your sister, and I want is that you----yes, you---have the chance to start

your own adventure----to do what fits you right.
Because, we really, really do love you.

        (Joey is perplexed. But then goes over to
        give his Father a long, intense HUG.)

                JUSTIN (almost crying)
I'm sorry. I really am.

                JOEY
You know, I now start to wake up better in the
morning. Maybe Jack and I might have something

                JUSTIN
Sure-----

                JOEY
But the people back at San Fran. My Sister----

                JUSTIN
It's your Mother, son. She would be really
upset if you did not comeback with me.

                JOEY
No, I cannot. That is all behind me now.

                JUSTIN
But you do not understand. Your Mother-----

                JOEY (angry)
My Mother and you do not run my life anymore!

                JUSTIN
Don't you care that she is extremely upset----

                JOEY
No. I can only care about my life now.

JUSTIN
Now you are talking a little like me now.
And I really do not think you mean that.

(Joey quickly walks over to the window now to
somewhat escape from his father.)

JOEY
No, you're right……but I do need what I have in
Montreal now…….but, but you're right……I really
do love my Mother……and I want so much to make
her happy.

JUSTIN
And you can always come back to this.

JOEY
But I just can't go back now------

JUSTIN
But your Mother, Joey. Thank about it. This was
her town as well. Every time you cross a new
street, you'll think about her-----and you'll
remember how guilty you felt because you didn't
go back to see her. Your Mother, Joey !!

(A brief pause)

JOEY
So when do you go back to the Bay area.

JUSTIN
Maybe the day after tomorrow. But it is
beautiful here. I'll have to hand it to you.
You do have good taste in cities. But I really
think you were chasing your Mother's roots.

(A long pause. Then Joey gets up and walks

to Justin.)

                    JOEY
I'm going back with you.

                    JUSTIN
You can come back in a few months. They'll all
be here.

                    JOEY
I'll get my things. Then we'll leave together.

        (Joey starts to walk to the door to exit.
        Justin looks straight at him.)

                JUSTIN (in gest)
Hey, Joey. (pause) I do not know how I can say
this.

                    JOEY
So go on.

                    JUSTIN
You'll think me a dirty ole man----

                    JOEY
What !!

        (There is a significant pause.)

                    JUSTIN
You look good. You really do.

        (Joey gives a quick wave, laughing, and
        then gives him the finger before he leaves.)

(BLACKOUT)

GAY FOR PAY   82

SCENE FIVE

The LaChine Canal Area in Montreal at
Dusk. Jack is standing on edge of the pier
overlooking two barges anchored to a small
dock. He is obviously enchanted by what he
sees, engulfed by the small breeze that comes
from the ever flowing body of water. He leans
against the steel railing.

       JACK (muttering to himself)
Beautiful. Magic colors----tranquil waters. Yet
I never Appreciated them at first. I thought
the waters muddy. But now (pause) Maybe they've
changed.

      (There is a slight pause. Then on the
      other end of the stage enters Marie Anne.
      She pretends to be quite surprised to see
      Jack.)

       MARIE ANNE (catty)
My God, what a coincidence. I didn't expect you
here. even though our office is not too far away.

       JACK (very stern)
I don't believe that Marie Anne. You are your
usual "snooping self."

       MARIE ANNE
No, I enjoy coming here a lot. More than you
do, perhaps. a little of Paris here with those
barges.

       JACK
I love Montreal. So glad I escaped to here.
Better than a lot of American ones.

(Suddenly Marie-Anne changes her tune.)

                    MARIE ANNE
C' est Samedi. I thought you would be with
Bill.

                    JACK
You mean Joey.

                    MARIE ANNE
That's Bill?

                    JACK
That's his real American name. He actually came
from San Francisco. I am sure he never told you
that.

                    MARIE ANNE
Really. Now I know that all American men are
liars.

                    JACK
You still tend to generalize too much. But you
still love them.

                    MARIE ANNE
Who cares what his name is. How between you
too.

                    JACK
Well, to answer your insatiable curiosity, he
does have very strong gay tendency. Yet he
still wants to make those videos.

                    MARIE ANNE
OK------

                         JACK
But all that is irrelevant now. Bill---Joey---
is returning to the States with his father.

                      MARIE ANNE
His father was here in Montreal?

                         JACK
My ex-lover ! Just arrived a few days ago. I
was---to say the least—surprised.

                      MARIE ANNE
I don't believe all this ! And you had sex with
his son.

                         JACK
True. PAID SEX.

                      MARIE ANNE
Your ex-lover must been very upset when he
knew you had a sexual relationship with his
son.

                         JACK
A gigolo relationship at that. But I did not
know Bill was his son. That made him very mad.
Made him vent a lot of words he never would
have said.

          (Marie Anne then takes a few steps away
          from Jack. Then turns back.)

                      MARIE ANNE
So you did have a close lover at one time.

                         JACK
My only one and last one.

(Marie Anne walks away from Jack, a little
perturbed)

MARIE ANNE
Why so stubborn. Why your age you Scared of
emotional involvement

JACK
As I told you before, it is a waste of time.
Too much emotional mess to clean up. You
never know what direction these relationships
move towards. At one moment you think you
are in control, then the next you lose out
completely---completely abandoned. That's
what I hate about them. (pause) But you know
what?

MARIE ANNE
Know what?

JACK
People spend a lot of time on these stupid
relationships. Trying to mold the other
person into someone who can adapt to your own
physical needs. Kind of selfish, don't you
think ?

MARIE ANNE
No. No selfish at all. We can not live without
those passionate feelings. That what life is
like. All ups and downs. Maybe that is what
God intended.

JACK
I'll have to speak to the Deity about that.
So what is your situation with Donny?

                        MARIE ANN

Ups and down. He still has the mentality of a
kid. He such a baby. But I like him so. I'm
trying to get him involved in a career. But I'm
trying to help him get a Work Visa. Or else
they might deport him.

                          JACK

Good luck.

                        MARIE ANN

But Jack, be open to a love relationship that
I know will come your way---without money. Deep
down inside, I know you really want it.

        (Jack starts to make a move to exit
        LaChine)

                          JACK

I don't know. Anyway, maybe we can do some work
tonight.

        (Marie Anne then stops Jack in his
        tracks.)

                        MARIE ANNE

Oh, Jack. One more thing.

                   JACK (stopping)

Yes.

                        MARIE ANNE

Be honest. I know you. Didn't you kinda know at
first that Bill was the son of your ex-lover?

        (There is a long pause. Jack obviously
        does not answer.)

                        JACK
You're being nosy again Marie Anne. (another
pause)

                     MARIE ANNE
Well !!

                        JACK
Come on. I can't answer that now-----

                     MARIE ANNE
Jack------JACK----- I know you.

        (After a pregnant pause)

                        JACK
I will tell you later when I am in a better
mood. Let's finish the budget.

        (Both Jack and Marie Anne walk off the
        stage together.)

                   THE END

Prop List:

Cereal boxes
Dishes
Portable Typewriter
Old pop-music magazines
Baseball hats
Towels
School notebook
Office briefcase
Alcohol drinking glasses
Coffee mugs
School backpack
Pens
VCR Player
Video Tape Cassettes
Old newspapers
Paper money
Cigarettes

Author's biography is at the end of this book.

ARLENE'S DESCENT

by Sal Anzalone

SYNOPSIS

Arlene Price never recovered from her Best Actress Oscar defeat twenty years ago. Determined to be celebrated and remembered by the Academy and her fans alike, Arlene begs her friend Jeff to write another script especially for her. There's one slight problem: the actress is beginning to show symptoms of dementia.

Arlene's Descent has been performed at St. Peter's in Manhattan under the direction of Sylvia Pilar. The play was later performed at Studio 353, courtesy of Genoveva Productions and directed by Julia Genoveva in Association with F.A.C.T. (Friends Always Creating Theatre).

CAST OF CHARACTERS

Arlene, early 70's-self-absorbed career-driven mature actress.
Jeff, mid 30's-Arlene's playwright/Screenwriter friend who indulges her.
Vito, early 60's-Jeff's blunt, opinionated and outspoken father.
Christina, early 30's-Arlene's transsexual son who prefers wearing dresses and makeup.

ARLENE'S DESCENT

ACT ONE

*Despite having mild dementia, actress **ARLENE PRICE** is obsessed with starring in one last movie before retiring. The setting is the actress's living room: there are bookcases, a sofa, two arm chairs, a coat rack, coffee table and maybe a fireplace. Part of her kitchen is in view-including her refrigerator. Arlene arranges flowers as her writer-friend **JEFF ROSSI** ENTERS. He holds a cake box and carries a briefcase. He takes out (of his briefcase) a script and a laptop and places them on the coffee table. He studies his cellphone closely.*

ARLENE I'm glad I made a key for you. *(Looking at cake box and script)* I see a cake box and script, but where's my laundry?

JEFF I thought laundry fell under the jurisdiction of Leon. *(Jeff picks up his cellphone to check for messages-much to Arlene's annoyance)* What happened to Leon? Did he get on your nerves?

ARLENE I let him go because… Let's just leave it at that.

    Jeff continues to focus on his phone.

ARLENE Are you expecting an impotent message?

JEFF *(Laughs)* No, I'm expecting a powerful,*capable* message.

ARLENE What?

JEFF You asked if I was expecting an *impotent* message.

ARLENE I said important, *not* impotent!

JEFF Sorry, my mistake.

ARLENE So are you?

JEFF Am I what?

ARLENE Expecting an important message?

JEFF My life's filled with great expectations.

ARLENE Is it possible to be more vague?

JEFF There's that spicy sarcasm your fans know nothing about.

ARLENE It's okay. I don't need to know. None of my business.

JEFF *(Beat)* Jennifer Aniston might buy my screenplay. She's supposed to give me an answer by the 15th. Her exact words were, "If I don't contact you by the 15th, assume I'm not interested."

ARLENE She's not interested. Now: Do you resent picking up my lasagna?

JEFF *Lasagna?*

ARLENE What lasagna? I said laundry.

JEFF I'm sorry. I could've sworn you said lasagna. Arlene, to be honest, I'd rather focus less on your errands and more on scripts. And speaking of scripts . . . In my possession is the play that'll resurrect your illustrious career! I finished it!

ARLENE Did you stop at the Post Office? Do I have parcels, correspondence-what's the word I want?

JEFF Mail.

> From his back pocket Jeff produces her
> mail, placing it on her coffee table.

ARLENE I don't know why I occasionally forget certain weather.

JEFF You forget certain *words,* not weather.

ARLENE Didn't I say *words*?

JEFF You said *weather.* *(Picks up script from coffee table and holds it like a mother holds an infant)*

ARLENE Let me have your latest creation!

> Jeff places script in Arlene's lap and places cake box in her refrigerator. Placing cake in her refrigerator, he finds ARLENE'S cellphone.

JEFF Thanks for having this little gathering. My Dad is a challenge, but lately he hasn't been well and I didn't want him to be alone on his birthday.

ARLENE Does he know what time to be here? How old is Victor now?

> She begins reading the play he brought.

JEFF *Vito* is 66. I told him eight o'clock. *(Jeff holds up her cellphone)* Tell me what your phone was doing in your refrigerator.

ARLENE I put it in the refrigerator because when it's beside me I habitually check for messages. If it's away, I'm not the least bit curious about who tasted me.

JEFF Tasted you or TEXTED you?

ARLENE I said texted!

JEFF *(chuckles)* I could've sworn you said TASTED. *(Smiles)* Between you and me, when *was* the last time somebody *tasted you*?

ARLENE New Year's Eve. It began with a long kiss and ended with... I can't discuss it. I might get aroused and end up making unwelcome advances. If only you were straight . . . *(Finally notices her phone in Jeff's hand)* I'll take that! *(Takes back her phone)*

JEFF Your phone needs defrosting. The truth Arlene: Did you put your phone in the fridge on purpose or did you—

ARLENE Did I *what?*

Doorbell rings

ARLENE Would you get that, darling?

*Jeff opens the door, **VITO**, JEFF'S father, a man of 66, ENTERS looking glum. He stamps his feet to wipe the snow off his shoes and removes his coat by placing it on a coat rack.*

JEFF Happy birthday, Dad!

VITO What's Norma Desmond reading over there?

JEFF The play I wrote for her.

Groaning, VITO collapses on sofa. ARLENE continues reading, ignoring VITO.

JEFF *(to Vito)* I'll make your birthday drink. What would you like?

VITO I'd like a new body. *(Sighs deeply)* Scotch, vodka-anything to help me forget I have pancreatic cancer.

JEFF prepares drink.

JEFF You don't have pancreatic cancer.

VITO I've Googled my symptoms. I have all the signs: I'm over 60, diabetic, smoke and have lower back pain. I'm no idiot.

JEFF hands VITO a drink and sits beside him.

VITO *(Cont'd)* Dr. Catalano wouldn't have made me undergo ultrasounds and blood tests without being suspicious. The worst part is the mortality rate. Only ten percent survive more than a year. *(Groans)* Obviously God's punishing me for what I did to you.

JEFF What did you do-besides give me an inferiority complex all of my life?

VITO From now on I'm going to try to pretend I approve of your life- just like your mother did. *(Looks up)* May she rest in peace. I think I'll be joining her soon.

JEFF *(Anxious to change topic)* My friend Lou Santoro may come by later. You'll like him: He's *Italian.*

VITO Who's Lou Santoro?

JEFF He was my boss at Chase. He's the only boss who tolerated my creative writing during company time. I'll always bend over backwards for him-even now that he's married.

VITO To a woman or a man?

JEFF To a woman. He has two sons.

VITO It's good you got at least one normal friend.

JEFF What do you mean, *normal?*

VITO He's not gay.

JEFF No, he's bisexual. *(Jeff's phone rings. Jeff checks phone, then answers)* Hi Lou. *(Beat)* I can't blame you. This is supposed to be one wicked blizzard. *(Beat)* I miss you too. *(Beat)* Okay, I will. Bye. *(Hangs up)*

VITO Was that the bisexual?

JEFF Yes.

VITO Do you have sex with him?

JEFF Yes, I do.

VITO What about his wife?

JEFF No, I *don't* have sex with his wife.

VITO Smartass. Does his wife know about you?

JEFF Yes, she knows about me. Lou and Lisa have an open relationship. She's also bisexual, by the way.

VITO You said he's *Italian?*

JEFF He's so Italian he eats spaghetti and meatballs every Sunday and has cannoli's and espresso for dessert.

> ARLENE drops the script she's reading and finally addresses VITO.

ARLENE Well, if it isn't Jeffrey's father. Happy birthday, Victor!

VITO It's *VITO.*

ARLENE I meant to say Vito.

VITO *(Rolls his eyes)* Did you know my son has a friend who doesn't appreciate his wife?

> ARLENE scoffs, picks up script and resumes reading.

JEFF *(to Vito)* He appreciates his wife!

VITO If he sees you, he doesn't appreciate her. Faggots I understand. I can't stand men who have sex with men AND women. They're half regular and half irregular.

JEFF There's no one quite like you, Dad. Thank God.

VITO Did his wife ever meet you?

JEFF No.

VITO It's disgusting that he cheats on his wife.

JEFF How can it be cheating if she knows about me? It's NOT cheating! *(Arlene senses an argument)*

ARLENE What's the problem?

JEFF No problem. Keep reading. I'm anxious to find out if you like it. While you read, I'll entertain my father by singing "YMCA" and "It's Raining Men."

VITO Your friend Lou is not a normal husband and his wife's not normal, either. It's a perverted, twisted marriage.

ARLENE Tell me Jeff: Does Lou love his wife?

JEFF Yes. In theatrical terms, his wife is his leading lady and I'm just the supporting actor. It's not a traditional marriage, but the two of them make it work.

ARLENE That's all that matters. Now: I MUST get back to your play. I like the title: "Miss Beverly Hills Has Arrived"

ARLENE continues reading.

VITO Your friend and his wife are making a mockery of the institution of marriage. It's wrong, if you ask me.

JEFF Nobody asked you.

VITO *(Groans)* I shouldn't give a shit about who you have sex with. I have bigger worries. I never thought cancer would claim my life. Years ago I went to a fortune teller who predicted I'd die of a heart attack at 94. That charlatan gave me inaccurate information. Instead of dying at 94, I'll die of cancer at 66.

ARLENE You have cancer?

VITO I'm sure of it.

JEFF He's speculating. He's a semi-hypochondriac.

VITO Better than being a semi-faggot like your married friend.

ARLENE Jeff, would you fix me a vodka and cranberry?

JEFF First tell me what you think of the script.

ARLENE I need a drink before I discuss your work.

> JEFF starts to stand, VITO pushes him down.

VITO I'll make it. Keeping busy helps me to not think about my death sentence. *(Sighs)* Of all cancers, why did it have to be pancreatic?

ARLENE Stop! If you have negative thoughts, keep them to yourself. It doesn't do any good to wallow in . . . *(looks lost)* misery. No! *(Beat)* Self-misery! *(Looks at Jeff)* What phrase am I looking for?

JEFF Self-pity.

ARLENE Yes! Self-pity! *(to Vito)* You are not to think of bad scenarios. *(to Jeff)* Speaking of bad, your play . . .

JEFF My play's bad? You don't like the part of Beverly?

ARLENE Beverly has too many lines! The play's not bad, but . . . *(Sighs)* I can't act in it. Not in my condition.

JEFF What condition?

ARLENE I don't want to get into it. *(Rises and paces sipping drink)* I have a wonderful idea. What if-

VITO -What time is your-

ARLENE Don't interrupt! Now I forgot my idea! *(to Jeff)* Sweetie: Is it possible to let Beverly ponder, laugh and cry a lot?

JEFF I *could*, but there has to be plausible reasons for her to ponder, laugh and cry.

VITO *(to Jeff, under his breath)* This actress has dementia and doesn't want to face it.

ARLENE What did he just say?

JEFF He asked me if later he can stream *Sensitive People.* He thinks you were magnificent in it.

ARLENE *(Smiles with pride)* I screamed so much in that film I couldn't speak for two weeks. Do you know I scream better than any actress- living *or* dead? *(She screams. Jeff and Vito applaud)* I still have it, don't I?

JEFF Yes, you do.

ARLENE So, in addition to my laughing and crying, I'd like to scream and ponder- especially ponder.

JEFF Why this sudden urge to ponder?

ARLENE It's not an urge. It's a visual gift to my audience. I'll wear something incredibly sensuous. I'll slowly stride upstage left to downstage right-giving my audience the privilege of undressing me with their curious and hungry eyes.

JEFF If you cry, laugh, ponder and scream, it won't reduce the number of lines. You *do* realize that?

ARLENE Oh, phooey! *(Beat)* You *could* rewrite the play for me.

JEFF Why not study your part till it's memorized?

ARLENE I thought of a better idea! *(Beat)* Let's set up a teleprompter so I can read my lines-just in case.

JEFF Teleprompters, Arlene, are not used in theatre.

ARLENE The hell with doing a play! I've changed my mind. I want to remain a movie actress. Write me another movie that's as marvelous as *Sensitive People.*

JEFF For ten months you begged me to write a play. Now, out of the clear blue, you want to return to the screen!

ARLENE The best thing about making a film is having the luxury of 7 hours to learn 2 lines of dialogue. Yes! Another movie would be just the ticket! What possessed me to *want* to do a play at this stage in my career?! Absurd!

JEFF Seriously, Arlene: I spent months conceiving, plotting, editing and polishing. Now, after my exhaustive labor, you don't want to act in it! Frankly, I'm disappointed.

> ARLENE reaches for her checkbook and pen. She writes JEFF a check and hands it to him. The amount astonishes JEFF.

JEFF What's this for?

ARLENE It's for your time, energy and talent. Even though I don't want to act in it, you're entitled to get paid. I have a question.

> VITO'S cellphone rings-much to ARLENE'S annoyance.

ARLENE Phooey! That damn phone is a distraction!

VITO finally answers his phone.

VITO Hello? Yes. *(Beat)* Can you speak louder? *(Beat)* That's better. I was hoping you'd-

ARLENE *(Outraged)* Go into one of my rooms so I don't have to hear fucking conversations I don't want to hear! Oh, it's absolute hell dealing with common people!

JEFF Dad: Finish your phone conversation in another room.

Following his son's advice, VITO EXITS.

JEFF *(Still holding check)* What did you want to ask?

ARLENE Is that amount satisfactory?

JEFF Actually it's more than I deserve.

ARLENE Then it may interest you to know I'm prepared to pay twice that amount if you write me another screenplay.

Arlene drops her pen. Jeff picks it up and hands it to her

ARLENE Thank you.

JEFF Uh-huh.

ARLENE What did you say?

JEFF What are you talking about?

ARLENE I dropped my pen, you picked it up. I said "thank you" and you replied, "Uh-huh." You should have said, "You're welcome." But you didn't. You had the nerve to say Uh-huh.

JEFF So?

ARLENE "Uh-huh" is a very rude and improper version of the standard classic, "You're welcome."

JEFF I don't understand.

ARLENE Didn't your parents teach you manners? "Uh-huh" isn't as sincere as "You're welcome." The next time I say thank you, don't reply at all if you can't respond with "You're welcome." I *loathe* people who utter "Uh-huh."

JEFF You win. Next time I'll reply with "You're welcome." Are you satisfied?

ARLENE Yes, I am. Thank you!

JEFF Uh-huh.

   ARLENE shoots him a dirty look

ARLENE So: *will* you write me another movie?

JEFF There are millions of writers. Why *me*?

ARLENE You brought me luck 20 years ago with *Sensitive People.* Audiences fell in love with my character. For two glorious months after the nominations were announced, the world hypothesized that I might win "Best Actress in a Leading Role." For two months I was the topic of discussion. It was wonderful! Finally, it was Oscar night. When the envelope was opened and my name *wasn't* announced, I smiled and appeared graceful but inside I died. I hated Meryl Streep for winning!

JEFF I'm missing your point.

ARLENE My point is, my intuition tells me if *you* write me another screenplay, I'll get nominated-and finally win. What's wrong with wanting to win?

JEFF Isn't it an honor to be *nominated*? Think of the hundreds of actors who've never been nominated and deserved to be!

ARLENE How can I make you understand? *(Closes*

eyes, opens eyes) Being nominated is like foreplay, but winning is sexual intercourse. I've been nominated and the foreplay was nice, but now I want to experience orgasm. *(Beat)* Write me another screenplay. I don't want to badger you, but *please* do.

JEFF Every dollar I earn these days is for my liver transplant. Without health insurance money has become a matter of life and death. I'm like 56 on the donor list. With a lot of money and some luck, I could be in the top 20. God, I sound more like a hit song than a liver recipient!

ARLENE So that's yes?

JEFF Yes.

> VITO RE-ENTERS, putting away his cellphone.

VITO I love Doctor Catalano. I say that in a pure male-bonding way, not in a homosexual way. He called to tell me I have a peptic ulcer. He didn't wanna wait until Monday to give me the results 'cause he knew how worried I was. What a relief!

ARLENE I'm glad you don't have that dreaded disease.

JEFF So much for self-diagnosis.

VITO On Monday I have to pick up medicine and go on a special diet, but tonight I eat and drink whatever the fuck I want to celebrate my rebirth! So: who wants another drink?

ARLENE I'll take another vodka and cranberry.

VITO You got it!

VITO prepares drinks.

VITO What time we eatin'?

ARLENE When my son gets here.

VITO hands ARLENE her drink.

VITO What's his name?

ARLENE Christina.

VITO Your son has a girl's name?

JEFF Oh, Lord. *(Looks up)* Here it comes.

ARLENE Christopher has recently made a few discoveries about his . . . identity.

VITO What do you mean, identity?

ARLENE He identifies as female.

VITO Hold it. If he was born a male, how can he identify as female?

ARLENE Being male isn't conductive- No, not *conductive!* What word do I want? *(Looks at JEFF)*

JEFF Conducive.

ARLENE Being male isn't *conducive* for him. *(To JEFF)* What would I do without you? *(To VITO)* My son identifies as a female.

VITO So he thinks he's a woman?

JEFF Oh, boy. Maybe I should say, "Oh, girl"

ARLENE He *knows* he's not female, but he *identifies* as a female.

VITO He's nuts.

ARLENE As a matter of fact, he often wears women's clothing. Gowns and dresses, mostly.

VITO Does he have the hots for men or women-or is he like Jeff's friend-who has the hots for anyone on two legs?

JEFF *(Sarcastically)* This'll be a *fun* evening!

ARLENE My Christopher is attracted to men.

VITO Another faggot who dresses like a woman!

JEFF The word is gay. He's gay. I mean *she's* gay.

VITO Christina is a fag. You may not like that word, but it was around long before you and me was born.

ARLENE I prefer you not use that word.

JEFF Dad: the drink you're holding-that'll be your last drink for tonight.

VITO I drink whatever the hell I want, whenever I want it. *(Beat)* Look: women who dress like men and men who dress like women . . . it's sick; it's wrong.

JEFF You may not think they deserve to choose their identity but their obligation isn't to you, their obligation is to *themselves.*

VITO Look: If you're born a man, you stay a man! If you're born female, you remain female. End of discussion.

ARLENE I never realized the extent of your ignorance. What don't you understand about transgenders and transvestites?

VITO Look: I'm a man. The world sees me as a man regardless of whether I identify myself as Spiderman, Superman, Ricky Ricardo or Mickey Mouse.

JEFF Get to the point, Dad.

VITO Shut up and listen. To me, identifying is another word for impersonating. *(Looks at ARLENE)* You're an actress. Can you play Billie Holliday if you *identify* as a black woman? No! Imagine Denzel Washington playing John F.

Kennedy because he "identifies" as a white male. It's dumb to identify with someone not of your race, and it's dumb to identify with someone not of your gender. *(Grunts)* I'm going to the bathroom now-not to do number two as *myself*, but to do number two as Robin from *Batman* because I identify as Robin. You know why? I can say, "Holy crap, Batman! *(Chuckles)*

    VITO EXITS.

JEFF On behalf of my father, I apologize. I wish his doctor had waited until Monday to give him his prognosis. He might've kept his unpopular opinions to himself.

ARLENE His opinions, unfortunately, are shared by the majority of the public. *(ARLENE stands and pours a drink)* Including me.

JEFF *(Stunned)* Including *YOU?*

ARLENE I'm . . . I'm ashamed to have a crossdresser for a son.

JEFF But he-*she*- obviously prefers wearing women's clothing and identifies as female. What's wrong with that?

ARLENE *(Returns to her chair)* I gave birth to a male. I named him Christopher. To make Christopher happy . . . Not "happy" *(Beat)* To please him. *(Sighs in frustration)* Not *please*. Placate? Oh, why do words fail me?

JEFF To appease him.

ARLENE *(Smiles)* Yes! To *appease* Christopher I'm forced to refer to him as Christina. I must be so careful what prophylactic I use. Not prophylactic! *(Sighs)* To be honest, I walk on eggshells every time he visits. That's a huge emotional burden for a mother.

VITO RE-ENTERS.

VITO What's a huge emotional burden for a mother?

ARLENE I was telling Jeff it's hard to adjust to the perception of Christopher as a female. I have trouble with *he* and *she*. What do you call those? Proteins? Prolapse? *(Smiling)* Pronouns!

VITO Does your son have a cock or a twat?

JEFF Quit being vulgar, Dad!

ARLENE Sexual reassignment hasn't taken place.

VITO What does *that* mean?

JEFF *(to Vito)* Christina has a penis.

VITO Wait, wait. So Christina has a penis and wears dresses?

ARLENE Yes.

VITO Does he wear dresses every day?

ARLENE Not *every* day. It depends on his mood.

VITO Maybe he's a bipolar drag queen with multiple personalities. What happens if he gets aroused in pants? Isn't it strange for a woman to have a hard-on?

JEFF The word is erection, Dad. You had them when you were *young*. Face facts: the world has changed since you were twenty-five.

VITO When I was 25 a man was born a man and *remained* a man-even if he wasn't happy about it. It was a better world.

ARLENE *(to JEFF)* I don't care for your father's crass manner, but I do share his opinion. I gave birth to a BOY. Though I pretend I support his choice, the reality is, I'm ashamed to have a son who impersonates a female. When I named him Christopher, I expected him to remain Christopher. My husband died when Chris was 9. At least he was spared the humiliation of witnessing his son change into his daughter. As his mother, I know I'm expected to be supportive, but it's hard to pretend I'm okay with his new identity when I'm NOT okay with it.

VITO Come on! You're an actress. You're a master at pretending! *(He rises to bar section)* Can I get anybody another drink? Me myself, I'm having another screwdriver!

JEFF Dad, you've had *enough*.

VITO Afraid I'll tell the truth? *(Beat)* There's no food out. I'm starvin'!

ARLENE When Christina gets here we'll eat.

Doorbell sounds

JEFF Dad, you're already up. Can you get the door?

VITO No way! I have a good idea of who it'll be.

*ARLENE rises and opens door. **CHRISTINA** ENTERS. She is a transgender woman who possesses a **semi masculine appearance**. She's not in the same league as Ru Paul or Caitlin Jenner. ARLENE hugs CHRISTINA and wipes snow from CHRISTINA'S coat. CHRISTINA removes her coat. She clutches a large handbag and carries it wherever she goes.*

ARLENE Christina: I love your outfit! Where did you get boots with pink heels? They're stupendous!

VITO *(to JEFF)* She's some actress!

ARLENE *(Points to JEFF)* I think you already know Jeff. *(Points to VITO)* I don't believe you met his father, Vito. *(She flashes a superficial smile at Vito)* Vito: this is Christina. By the way: today is Vito's birthday!

CHRISTINA *(to VITO)* Happy birthday! *(Sits next to VITO)* You don't mind if I take off my boots, my feet are aching from these heels!

> CHRISTINA removes her boots. VITO looks at her as if she has two heads. It's obvious he's uncomfortable; he's never seen a trans- gender woman up-close.

VITO Finally. Now we can eat!

CHRISTINA Not until I have a couple of tall drinks.

VITO *I* was here on time. I *already* had a couple of tall drinks.

CHRISTINA Good for you. I can use a stiff one. *(Smiles at JEFF)* You'll do nicely. But for now I'll settle for a drink.

JEFF I'll make it. What's your pleasure?

CHRISTINA You! *(Smiles)* Not only are you handsome, you're a gentleman. I'll take a Greyhound.

JEFF That's a bus line and a dog breed, not a drink!

VITO Greyhound is grapefruit juice with vodka. *(to CHRISTINA)* How can you go out in public dressed like that? If you want to dress like a woman, do it in private. The rest of us don't want to see you dressed like a damn broad.

CHRISTINA Are you a new arrival to Earth? What planet are you from?

VITO The female impersonators I respected were on *The Ed Sullivan Show*. Jim Bailey and Charles Pierce looked like honest-to-goodness dames. I accepted them. But amateurs should never appear in public. If I can tell you're a man under all the make-up-and I do-- you've failed my test. And if you fail my test, you're a fraud, a freak.

CHRISTINA Oh, I see: If we're professionals, we're accepted. If we're non-professionals, we're freaks.

VITO You got that right.

JEFF That's the same logic Zack McGovern has.

ARLENE Who's Zack McGovern?

JEFF My father's friend who only respects talented, famous blacks like Johnny Mathis, Diana Ross, Oprah and Sidney Poitier. He refers to them as "talented and distinguished black artists."

ARLENE What-I'm afraid to ask-does he call blacks who aren't talented and distinguished?

VITO I'll give you one guess.

CHRISTINA *(Clears throat)* So how old are you on this birthday of yours?

ARLENE It's not polite to ask a man his age.

CHRISTINA I'm not asking a man, I'm asking a Neanderthal.

VITO I'm proud to be 66.

CHRISTINA How can you be proud to be so old?!

JEFF, who's been fixing drinks hands one to CHRISTINA.

CHRISTINA Thanks. By the way, I'd love to jump your bones. You're hot.

JEFF Speaking of hot, I better check the food.

CHRISTINA Take your time. I want to down a few drinks before I sit down to dinner.

JEFF Dad: I need your help. Come into the kitchen with me.

VITO I don't feel like rising.

CHRISTINA It's alright not to rise. *(JEFF EXITS)* What's not alright is not being able to *get it up*. *(Looks at VITO)* I understand men of your age usually come DOWN with that affliction. *(Giggles)* Oh, listen to me: I made a joke. I swear I didn't plan on saying "come down." The words came out so natural.

VITO What do *you* know about *natural?*

CHRISTINA Excuse YOU?

VITO You're very outspoken.

CHRISTINA Are you bothered by outspoken women?

VITO Not if they're GENUINE women. I am bothered by comments from *freaks* like you.

> CHRISTINA laughs to hide her hurt. ARLENE breaks the tension.

ARLENE Did I tell you that Jeff has agreed to write a screenplay especially for me?

CHRISTINA So, "Grandpa": What makes you think I'm a freak?

VITO You appear to be half female and half male.

ARLENE You MUST leave. I've had enough of your incest. Insubordination. No! *(Closes eyes, opens eyes)* Insensitivity!

> VITO rises.

VITO Before I go, you should know that what

makes you a freak more than anything else is the fact that nobody wants you.

CHRISTINA What do you mean?

VITO Exactly what you think I mean. Freaks like you are welcome nowhere.

ARLENE My Christina is welcome everywhere.

VITO *(to CHRISTINA)* Not in the men's and ladies' rooms!

> VITO struts to doorway but before he reaches door, CHRISTINA confronts him.

CHRISTINA For your information, caveman, I'm welcome in all restrooms throughout these United States.

> Itching for a fight, VITO briskly returns to his seat.

VITO Who told you *that*-Cher's off-spring or the woman once known as Bruce Jenner? I'm telling you that you're welcome nowhere. Women are ill-at-ease seeing a makeshift female with a penis and for good reason: you're *not* a natural woman.

ARLENE *(Trying to break the tension)* What a beautiful song: "Natural Woman" Did Aretha Franklin write AND sing that or just sing it? I met Aretha at a party years ago. She wore a red dress and gave me unforgettable career advice. Unfortunately I've forgotten the advice.

VITO *(Back to CHRISTINA)* Anybody with a deep voice who enters the men's room in a dress with masculine arms, hands and legs and an Adam's apple is a freak.

CHRISTINA You're a genuine asshole!

VITO The only ones comfortable with your kind

are freaks like you. Look: if you have a vagina, use the ladies room; if you have a penis, use the men's room. If your parts are under construction, you're welcome nowhere.

CHRISTINA Your feeble mind can't fathom fluidity. You can't function in a world without labels. You're old and rigid. I don't like you!

JEFF RE ENTERS.

VITO *(to CHRISTINA)* You know why you don't like me? I tell the truth.

ARLENE Is the food ready?

JEFF The lasagna will take a while because somebody put the lasagna in her oven without turning the oven ON. *(Looks at Arlene harshly and sits)* So what did I miss?

CHRISTINA Just your father's ignorance.

VITO It's true.

CHRISTINA Congrats: I give you points for admitting you're ignorant.

VITO No. What's true is, I'm comfortable with labels. Let's take lasagna. I know what lasagna looks and tastes like 'cause I've tasted it before. When I'm given a menu, the foods are listed so when I order I know what I'll be served-and what I'll be eating.

CHRISTINA For your information, I'm not lasagna-although I am delicious. I'm not sure of many things, but I'm sure you'll never eat *me*. Intelligent people first taste something and then ask about its ingredients. *(to JEFF)* I'm willing to be *your* lasagna *anytime*. Whenever you're hungry, I'm willing to satisfy your appetite.

VITO Look: Very few men who fancy themselves as women look like genuine women. Most of them look like they're going to a damn masquerade party. I don't care what laws are passed. The court of public opinion says biologically born males who remodel themselves into women look like exhibits in circus side shows.

ARLENE *(Anxious to change subject)* Jeff: What kind of story will you write?

JEFF Something tailored to your unique talent.

VITO Years back I'd look at beautiful women with admiration. There was no scrutiny, no overthinking. Now when I'm attracted to a beauty I'm forced to wonder if she was born a woman. I don't wanna sleep with someone who was born a male and later became a female. Let's say I meet a woman at the opera . . .

JEFF You don't understand opera.

CHRISTINA And anything he doesn't understand he condemns!

VITO Suppose I meet a woman at a baseball game and she accepts my invitation to go to my place . . .

ARLENE Wouldn't that mean she struck out?

CHRISTINA That's a good one, Ma.

VITO Let's say we become intimate at my place. Today it wouldn't be shocking for a beauty to take off her clothes and whip out a dick. It works the other way, too: a man can look like a man and later confess his birth name is Mildred.

CHRISTINA That's unacceptable.

VITO *(Stunned)* You agree with me?

CHRISTINA Oh, yes: It's unacceptable for anyone to be called *Mildred.* It's a name from 1910 or something.

VITO My homo son is looking better.

JEFF Why am I looking better?

VITO Given a choice, I'll take a gay man who looks like a man over someone who leaves his house wearing a dress and make-up. *(to Christina)* Trans people make me sick!

> CHRISTINA rises, finds her boots and begins putting them on. She approaches doorway.

CHRISTINA If this birthday was guaranteed to be your last, I'd join in the celebration. *(She puts on her coat)*

ARLENE Don't go.

JEFF Don't let my old man get to you. You can't leave in a blizzard!

VITO He's leaving because he can't bear the truth!

JEFF *"She's* leaving."

ARLENE If anyone should leave, Victor, it's YOU.

VITO I'm Vito! *(to CHRISTINA)* I was born a *he* and I'll remain a *he* till I die. That's how it should be!

ARLENE *(to VITO)* The problem isn't your gender; the problem is that you were born at all! Take yourself into the kitchen so you're not seen or heard!

> VITO rises and keeps a low profile for the time being.

JEFF *(to CHRISTINA)* Sit and relax. My father

doesn't know any better. Until he met my mother, he lived in a large cave.

CHRISTINA smiles, removes her coat and returns to her seat.

JEFF *(Cont'd)* What can you say about a man whose TV hero is Archie Bunker? He doesn't know a lot.

CHRISTINA He doesn't know anything!

Vito stands in a corner and slowly makes his way back to his seat.

VITO I know that people are hypocrites. They agree with my opinion but they're afraid to admit it. They don't want to be accused of transphobia. They'll tell you they have no problem with trans people and transvestites. But what they're thinking is, "Trans people are sick."

CHRISTINA Is that *all* they think?

VITO You were born with a penis, damn it! You can tuck it away, cut it off or pretend it's a vagina. But your penis will never change into a vagina that sex symbols like Marilyn Monroe, Liz Taylor and Lana Turner were born with.

CHRISTINA *(Outraged)* Those are dead sex symbols-dead like your imagination. Old man: you live in the past. Forget Marilyn, Liz and Lana. Focus on someone like Caitlyn Jenner 'cause she's alive and she matters more than you do!

VITO *(Equally outraged)* No matter what amount of surgery you undergo, the only gender that matters is the one that's on your birth certificate!

CHRISTINA No. What matters is the one *I* identify with.

ARLENE Let's eat spaghetti!

JEFF Lasagna.

CHRISTINA Give her a break: they're both Italian and made with tomato sauce. *(to JEFF)* What do you think? Do you think trans people are strange or freakish? I could use your support.

VITO If you want support, wear a bra. *(Laughs)*

ARLENE Jeff gets quiet sometimes. He suffers from social awkwardness. *(Beat)* Social isolation. No, not that one. He has-

VITO Social anxiety! *(Looks at JEFF)* Or are you an introvert with a side order of social anxiety? *(Laughs)*

JEFF Thanks, Dad. If there's one thing introverts love it's being forced into the spotlight.

VITO He loves emailing more than using his phone. He thinks everyone's hanging on to his every word.

CHRISTINA *(to JEFF)* What kind of things are difficult for you?

ARLENE Hateful confrontations at social gatherings?

Remaining silent, JEFF nods head in agreement

ARLENE *(Cont'd)* Jeff prefers his laptop for company. Being surrounded by people he doesn't know well makes him uneasy.

VITO He knows you pretty well, but as far as your son is concerned-

CHRISTINA I'm her daughter, *not* her son! Everyone better start referring to me as *she*.

VITO I'd rather not refer to you at *all*.

CHRISTINA I read where introverts hate small

talk. They don't see the point in small talk. They view it as forced conversation. Introverts don't feel the need to say everything they think or share every emotion they feel.

JEFF It's true. I'd rather write a script or compose an email than have face-to-face conversations.

ARLENE Really?

VITO Introverts would rather write than talk.

CHRISTINA *(to JEFF)* I wish your father was an introvert. To not see and hear him would be awesome. That's my wish.

VITO *(to CHRISTINA)* My wish is that you look like a man, but hey: life's full of disappointments!

CHRISTINA Old men like you think in black and white. Everyone has to be male or female. Those rules you learned when Abe Lincoln was your President are outdated! We-the young- have our own game with our own rules. The more you resist, the more you'll appear foolish, inflexible and weird.

VITO You- a man dressed like a woman-you're telling me that *I'm* weird?! Let me ask you something. Do you expect to fall in love?

CHRISTINA Yes.

VITO With a man?

CHRISTINA Of course with a man; I'm not a lesbian.

VITO You think a man is gonna accept your female exterior along with your male interior?

CHRISTINA Yes, if he's unlike you.

VITO What do you mean, unlike me?

CHRISTINA Unlike you is a man who's educated, sensitive and sophisticated. A man who values my inner beauty above my pretty face and youthful body which, in time, will fade.

VITO If you insist on being a fag, why not be a fag like my son? He's your typical faggot.

JEFF I'm not typical.

VITO *(to JEFF)* How are you not typical? Tell me. I may be disgusted by what I hear, but I'll allow it. Proceed.

CHRISTINA Thank you, Judge Ass-wipe!

JEFF I'm atypical 'cause I'm not a top or a bottom.

ARLENE What does top and bottom mean?

CHRISTINA In your case, 20 years ago you were on top, now you're at the bottom, career-wise.

JEFF A top is someone who *(Stops himself)* I can't say it; I can't bear his reaction. He might die of shock.

CHRISTINA *(Smiles superficially at VITO)* A top is someone who sticks his penis into his partner's rectum. A bottom is the one who receives the penis in his rectum.

VITO *(to JEFF)* If you don't do one or the other, what *do* you do?

JEFF I'm into frottage.

VITO *(to ARLENE)* Do you know what frottage is?

ARLENE It sounds like a side dish I'd serve with a broccoli quiche.

VITO What's frottage?

CHRISTINA It involves being face-to-face naked and rubbing your genitals against another man's genitals. It's popular among men who'd rather not engage in anal sex.

JEFF I'm thrilled someone has actually heard of it.

CHRISTINA It's supposed to be safer than penetration.

ARLENE Why do all gay men love penetration?

JEFF Not *all* gay men. For me, frottage is more pleasurable than penetration.

CHRISTINA I think your social anxiety days are limited!

JEFF During frottage, no hand to genital contact occurs. If you're face-to-face, you can French kiss-

CHRISTINA *(to VITO)* For your benefit, *caveman,* that means using tongue for kissing.

JEFF The sensation of two penises rubbing naked together can cause me to ejaculate.

ARLENE So frottage means direct penis-to-penis contact?

CHRISTINA Haven't you been listening? Yes.

JEFF Two penises coming together by mingling, caressing and sliding-with or without lubricant- is the most pleasurable feeling in the world.

VITO *(to JEFF)* Yuck! Listen to me: the most pleasurable feeling is the way your mother and me had sex. It was normal. It resulted in pregnancy. That's how you got here.

JEFF I appreciate being born, but I'm not returning the favor by reproducing. The family name will end after my death.

VITO I'd still take the way you are than have

you wear a dress and "identify as a woman" like this one *(looks at CHRISTINA)* over here.

CHRISTINA *(to VITO)* I'm trying to imagine you with a personality. *(Beat)* Your ignorant comments mean nothing. The only adult who matters to me is my mother. I can say with absolute certainty that she approves of me and she's proud of me exactly as I am.

VITO Are you sure about that?

ARLENE *(to CHRISTINA)* Of course I'm proud! *(Beat)* I think it's time for spaghetti to be served.

JEFF Lasagna.

ARLENE Whatever it is, we should consume it.

VITO Why don't you tell your precious baby how you *really* feel?

JEFF I need your help in the kitchen, Dad.

VITO Be quiet, Mr. Frottage. You're not even capable of having sex the way other faggots do! *(to ARLENE)* See how I'm not afraid to speak my mind? Jeff knows full well that I disapprove of him.

JEFF I've known it all my life. It's been a struggle to make my life work. Every time I hear a song with lyrics like "I love her" I change it to "I love HIM" so it fits into my life. I've always translated straight lyrics so I could feel included. That's why "How Deep Is Your Love" is one of my favorite songs. There's no gender mentioned in the lyrics.

VITO Give your opinion, Arlene. Don't be afraid.

ARLENE I don't know what you're talking about.

VITO Admit to Christina that you don't approve. Have the *balls*-excuse me. *(Beat)* Have the ovaries to tell Christina what you told us before he showed up!

CHRISTINA What was that?

ARLENE It's not important.

CHRISTINA Out with it, Ma.

> There's awkward silence. VITO breaks the silence.

VITO Your mother said she gave birth to a male. To appease you, she's forced to refer to you as Christina, and she doesn't like doing that.

> CHRISTINA looks at her mother with astonishment.

CHRISTINA *(to ARLENE)* Is this true?

> There's more awkward silence. ARLENE breaks the silence.

ARLENE I *may* have said words to that affect, but my opinion doesn't carry much weight. Your happiness is all that matters.

VITO She also said that-

ARLENE Stop being an instigator!

CHRISTINA It's okay. I want to hear everything. *(ARLENE rises to make another drink, she'll need it)* So what *else* did you say, Ma?

ARLENE It's *not* important.

CHRISTINA It's important to me.

ARLENE My memory is faulty. I can't recall every single word.

> There's another beat of silence until...

VITO She told us that she pretends to support you, but she's ashamed to have a son who impersonates a female. This is a quote: *(Clears throat)* "My late husband was spared the humiliation of witnessing his son change into his daughter. It's hard to pretend I'm okay with my son's new identity when I'm not okay with it."

JEFF Are you satisfied, Dad?

VITO Look: I may not have as many hard-ons as I once did, but I still got guts. A real man says what other men are too scared to say.

JEFF Is that what a real man is to you-a snitch?

ARLENE *(to VITO)* Your sarcasm, Jeff, is inadvisable. It's- *(Closes eyes, opens them)* Inappropriate. *(Sighs)* Thank God I remembered. Vito: you should thank God I don't carry a gun because if I did, you'd be dead. You had no right to repeat what I said!

CHRISTINA Then it *is* true.

> Looking grim, CHRISTINA rises, puts on her coat and approaches doorway.

ARLENE Where are you going?

CHRISTINA Anywhere but here.

ARLENE Don't be mad. Let's talk about it.

CHRISTINA You've already talked it out. I *know* how you feel. Want to deny what you said?

ARLENE *(After a few beats)* No.

> CHRISTINA inches closer to door.

ARLENE *(Desperate)* You can't go like this. You haven't eaten.

CHRISTINA I've lost my appetite.

ARLENE Please let me explain my feelings.

CHRISTINA *(Angry)* I know how you feel. That's precisely the problem!

ARLENE You shouldn't be mad at me. All I was doing was expressing MY opinion. *(Beat)* Actually, you should thank me.

CHRISTINA *(Incredulously)* For what? Disapproving of my life's choice? Are you out of what's left of your mind?

ARLENE *(Rises for dramatic effect)* My own mother disapproved of my wanting to act. She said I wasn't beautiful. She claimed women had to be beautiful to be successful actresses. I guess she never heard of Lily Tomlin. She told me I was neither beautiful nor talented. I remember her words: "Arlene, you'll never amount to anything" I've forgotten just about everything else, but not her emotionally shattering remarks. Oddly enough, they were the remarks that encouraged me to succeed. When she told me I'd never amount to anything, I was determined to never give up my dream. Use my disapproval of your cross dressing by becoming the most successful drag queen in the world! I want you to put Peter Paul to shame.

CHRISTINA *Who?*

ARLENE That drag queen: Peter Paul-like the company that makes *Almond Joy,* the coconut chocolates. *(Everyone looks confused)* The one with the drag race show: Peter Paul!

JEFF You mean *Ru Paul*?

ARLENE That's the one! I want you to put him to shame! When audiences see you, Christina, they must never see one iota of maleness. Let 'em all believe you have a vibrant vagina between your legs!

CHRISTINA I don't *want* to be an entertainer. I want to live my life as an ordinary woman.

ARLENE *(Shocked)* Ordinary woman? You certainly don't take after me. You have such modest expectations.

CHRISTINA So my grandmother disapproved of your acting ambition and you claim her put-downs made you a "screen legend." But what was good for you isn't good for me. I may sound secure and independent, but your disapproval has totally shattered me. *(Grabs coat and puts it on)*

ARLENE Come sit down and stop being so dramatic!

CHRISTINA No! I refuse to eat with people who are intolerant and transphobic. *(She positions herself at doorway)*

JEFF *(Rises, approaches CHRISTINA)* I'm not intolerant or transphobic. I know how it feels to have a parent disapprove of the way you live your life. Let's go somewhere and have a heart-to-heart.

CHRISTINA Of everyone here, you're my favorite-and not because you're handsome. Right now, though, I want to be alone. *(She opens door)*

JEFF But there's a serious blizzard happening.

CHRISTINA Yes- mostly in my head. All I know is, I can't be here-not while I'm feeling what I'm feeling. *(Beat)* I need to get out of here. But I better use the bathroom first. *(Turns to ARLENE)* May I use your bathroom, mother?

ARLENE Yes, you may. Later this week I want to have a good talk with you.

CHRISTINA All this time I was under the mistaken impression that I had your support, but I never did. You have no idea Ma, how low that makes me feel.

> CHRISTINA EXITS. JEFF returns to his chair.

VITO Well, let's eat!

JEFF Go in the kitchen and stay there! You deserve to be alone; this all happened because of your transphobic mouth.

ARLENE Ah, what's done is done. Sooner or later Christopher would've known my true feelings. *(to VITO)* Go make yourself a plate.

VITO If you two aren't eating, I'm not gonna eat.

JEFF *(to ARLENE)* He wants to stay so he can hear your every word so when Christina exits the bathroom, he can repeat every word to her.

VITO What does *that* mean?

> With his eyes, JEFF dismisses him.

ARLENE It'll take a while, but I'm sure he'll come around.

JEFF *She'll* come around. Arlene, you have to refer to Christina in female pronouns.

ARLENE It's okay now: he's not here. But you're right: I should get used to it whether he's here or not. *(Beat)* "*She's* here or not" *(Beat)* I can't remember simple pronouns and YOU want me to learn dialogue without cue cards!

> JEFF'S cellphone rings. He answers it.

JEFF Excuse me.

> *Jeff EXITS. ARLENE and VITO are alone*

ARLENE My next movie will be a hit. Do you know why?

VITO I'm sure you'll tell me.

ARLENE Your son's a talented writer-and I'll have every line of dialogue written out on cue cards like Marlon Brando did on the set of *The Godfather*. I'll be nominated and this time I'll win. Unless Meryl Streep gets nominated. *(Looks above)* Please, Lord, don't let her be nominated in my category! I want to win, damn it, win!

JEFF RE-ENTERS.

JEFF Do you know who I was talking to? Jennifer Aniston! She apologized for notifying me so late, but she wanted me to know she's considering two scripts: one from somebody else-whose name she won't divulge-and MY script! She and her agent are getting together to decide which script to go with.

VITO They're meeting in this awful weather?

JEFF In California it's a sunny 80 degrees. I can't believe it: Jennifer Aniston loves my screenplay!

VITO She also loves somebody else's screenplay. *(JEFF gives VITO a dirty look)* You've got a 50/50 chance she'll buy your story.

JEFF Thanks for the encouragement, Dad.

VITO All I'm doing is pointing out reality.

ARLENE *(to JEFF)* I was just telling your father that because of your brilliant writing, I'll be nominated for a Best Actress Oscar and I'll finally win!

JEFF I haven't started writing and already you're being nominated for an award? You're amazing.

ARLENE I believe in optimism.

JEFF I don't know why you're so intent on my writing it.

ARLENE I see what's happening. You're trying to back out of our deal. Now that Jennifer Jones . . . Jennifer Lopez . . . *Which* Jennifer is she?

JEFF Aniston.

ARLENE Now that Jennifer the Greek has shown interest in your script, you can't be bothered writing for little old *me*. She's the only one who matters. She's younger, prettier and more talented. *(Beat)* The least you can do is disagree with me! *(JEFF remains silent)* My worst fear is a CONDOM. No! Confounded. No. My worst fear has been *Confirmed.* You've lost interest in writing for me. I'm no longer news worthy. I'm a has-been. *(She returns to her seat)*

JEFF Not to worry. I'll create a magnificent script for you.

ARLENE You've just redeemed yourself. *(Smiles)* It was your baby, *Sensitive People* that earned me world admiration and recognition. I'm superstitious: I can't jinx my luck: You MUST write for me so lightning can strike twice in a lifetime.

JEFF I already agreed, remember?

ARLENE I know but I have to be sure. *(Beat)* I'm going to let you in on a secret...

JEFF With my Dad's big ears?

VITO rises, ready to exit.

VITO I can take a hint. I know when I'm not wanted.

JEFF No, you don't!

ARLENE I want to win an Oscar more than *anything.* *(Stands and paces)* I'd rather win an Oscar than live to be a hundred. I'd rather win an Oscar than have sex three times a week for as long as I live.

VITO Obviously you're more narcissistic than horny.

ARLENE *(Gives VITO a dirty look)* Keep quiet! This is *MY* scene. If someone came up to me and said, "Yes, Arlene, you'll win an Oscar, but it'll cost you a son: he'll die in a horrific car crash. Which is it, Arlene? Win an Oscar or have your son die?" Believe it or not, I'd choose an Oscar!

JEFF *(to Vito)* Did you commit Arlene's words to memory? When Christina comes back out I'm sure you'll repeat what Arlene said-you tattletale.

VITO You're a smart-ass!

JEFF I'm not sure my ass is smart, but I am blessed with a firm bubble-butt.

ARLENE In my obituary, I want them to write, "She won an Oscar." Know why? It's fucking hard to win an award. If they write, "Arlene has a son" people will say, "So what? Millions of women have sons, but very few women have-

VITO -have sons who dress up like girls! *(laughs)*

JEFF *Women*, Dad, not girls. Maybe if more sons dressed like women, they'd behave as sensibly as women- which would result in less violence. More men than women commit violence and murder.

VITO What about Katherine the Great, Lizzie Borden and Lana Turner?

ARLENE Lana Turner! *(Arlene returns to her seat)*

VITO She killed that gangster: Johnny something-or-other.

JEFF That was self-defense. Granted, some women do commit murders and are as inconsiderate as men, but most are decent. Maybe that's why Christina identifies as one.

ARLENE So, dear heart: when will you start writing my movie?

> JEFF'S cellphone rings. He answers.
> Wanting privacy, he EXITS.

VITO *(to ARLENE)* It's bad enough that Jeff's a homo, but did it ever occur to you that maybe he's lost his creative juices? It's been 20 years since he wrote *Sensitive People.*

> JEFF RE-ENTERS looking depressed.

JEFF Jennifer decided to go with someone else's script.

VITO Did she tell you who the other writer is?

JEFF What difference does it make? It's not me.

ARLENE I'm sorry Jennifer ANACIN didn't pick your script, but look at the bright side: you still get to write for me and you know I pay very well.

VITO I bet if you weren't a homo, Jennifer would've picked your script.

JEFF I'm sure that's the reason. *(rolls his eyes)*

VITO Maybe I'll have something to eat.

> VITO rises and EXITS.

JEFF I want to apologize. My father had no right to repeat to Christina what you—

ARLENE —No need to apologize. As I said, Christina had to learn my feelings eventually. Congratulate me: I said Christina instead of Christopher. See, I'm learning. (Beat) I wish he-*she*- wasn't so sensitive. She may not talk to me for some time. But I'm sure my performance-in your screenplay will reduce her to tears.

> VITO RE-ENTERS holding a plate of lasagna and a piece of bread.

VITO Who's in tears?

ARLENE *(Rises, paces theatrically)* My riveting performance in the movie Jeff writes will render everyone misty-eyed *(Beat)* Phooey! I could've won 20 years ago if that bitch didn't pick MY year to deliver one of her overrated performances. Why can't I remember her name?

VITO Because you've got dementia-which is why you should retire.

JEFF Dad, she doesn't have dementia.

ARLENE Yes, I do.

JEFF This is the first time I've heard you admit it.

ARLENE My having that dreadful disease is why I MUST get another Oscar nomination and win. Time's running out. I must taste victory before it's too late. The feeling of winning an Oscar is better than great sex.

VITO How do you know? You haven't won an Oscar.

JEFF I thought you were going to say she never experienced great sex! Arlene, in all seriousness: Why would you *want* to make another movie when in a few years you may not know your own name?

ARLENE *(Sighs deeply)* In time I may not know my name, but luckily audiences *will*. They don't have that dreadful disease that robs them of communication and cognition. *(She rises and paces)* I want to please them. Every move I make is for my public. I live for my fans. It's unlikely I'll ever be fucked again and it's unlikely I'll reach my one-hundredth birthday. My one remaining goal is to be celebrated as I should've been long ago. That I didn't win the first time was a travesty of justice. There haves been past mistakes: Diana Ross should've won for *Lady Paints the Blues*, not Liza for *Cabaret*. Al Pacino should've won for *Dog Day Night*, not for-what was the movie they gave him an Oscar for years later?

VITO *Scent of a Woman.*

JEFF That was a good movie, but NOT his best.

VITO It *was* his best! You don't like it 'cause the scent of a woman makes you throw up. If it was called *Scent of a Man* you'd love it. Al Pacino: *that's* what I call a real man-unlike you.

JEFF Fuck you, Dad. I'm a real man.

VITO *(Rises with anger)* You're not. If you were, you wouldn't be sleeping with men. Real men desire real women. Subject closed!

JEFF Why are you so damn angry?

VITO Because you're my son you should want women! You're not normal! *(Sighs and sits)* I'm sorry. *(Looks at JEFF)* I am angry. How did you know?

JEFF It's obvious. What's bothering you?

VITO Only someone of my age would understand. You wouldn't understand.

JEFF Try me.

VITO I'm not angry at you. I'm not even angry with female impersonators. It's that . . . my life is almost over and I haven't done half the things I wanted to do. One of my ambitions is to rebuild my '57 Chevy Belair. In my mind I think I have plenty of time, but I don't. *(Looks at JEFF)* I'm jealous of you-and everyone your age. You'll all be around for a long time. *(Rises and paces)* I may not have cancer right now, but my time is limited and I'm NOT ready to go. I still want someone to love me. I want to fall in love one more time before I call it a life. But because *I* want it doesn't mean it'll happen. *(Looks at Jeff)* It doesn't matter who you love. What matters is that you're loved. I'm in the winter of life and I'll never find someone who'll love me like your mother did. I wish I were your age. *(Beat)* Before Christina leaves I want to apologize to her for all the things I said.

JEFF How long has Christina been in the bathroom?

ARLENE He-*she's* been in there too long.

> *ARLENE rises and EXITS. Seconds later, ARLENE screams.*

VITO Was that her real scream or is she rehearsing her famous scream?

JEFF That was real.

> JEFF EXITS leaving VITO alone. After a beat, ARLENE and JEFF RE-ENTER. ARLENE looks grief stricken; JEFF escorts her to her seat. ARLENE sobs.

VITO What's the matter?

> There's silence. After a beat . . .

JEFF Christina killed herself. She took about 30 Xanax.

VITO What?!

ARLENE *(She cries)* Why, why, why!

JEFF Obviously she's been unhappy for a long time.

VITO I got to see this for myself.

> VITO rises and EXITS

ARLENE I never thought he'd take his life. Was it my fault, Jeff?

> JEFF remains silent. VITO RE ENTERS holding a note.

VITO He left a note. Take a look at this.

> JEFF grabs the note out of VITO'S hand. JEFF reads note.

ARLENE (to *VITO)* Get me a drink.

VITO What would you like?

ARLENE Anything-just be quick about it!

> VITO prepares her a drink as ARLENE continues crying. He hands drink to her.

JEFF I think you should read this.

ARLENE *(Shakes her head)* I can't. *You* read it for me.

> ARLENE guzzles her drink quickly (believing she'll be able to cope better if she's drunk.) VITO returns to his seat next to JEFF.

JEFF *(reading CHRISTINA'S suicide note)* "When I first learned what transgender meant

I was elated. After years of confusion I
finally understood who I was. I had hoped my
mother would be supportive. Tonight, quite by
accident, I learned she's ashamed of me. As a
sensitive person, I care what my mother thinks.
I've craved for her approval but I've been
disappointed. Therefore I'm checking out of
this hypocritical world. Tonight's revelation
was too much. I refuse to suffer mental anguish
brought on by unenlightened, callus people--
including my mother. She's never been nurturing
or caring. She's nothing more than a career.
I long for peace, and death is the only way.
(JEFF looks at ARLENE) It's signed Christina.

ARLENE He did it to hurt me.

JEFF What?

ARLENE Christopher wanted to hurt me.

VITO We have to call 911, right?

ARLENE Not until I decide how I'm going to play
the scene.

JEFF What scene?

ARLENE With any luck, Christopher's death
can work to my advantage. My fans might have
sympathy for me. This tragedy has the potential
to elevate my waning celebrity status. I want
my public to know how very close Christopher
and I were.

JEFF You weren't close.

ARLENE But the public doesn't know that. Let me
see the note he left.

> JEFF hands her the suicide note. ARLENE
> rips it to shreds.

ARLENE *(to JEFF)* When the ambulance, cops and
media circus arrives, do me a favor: Tell

them Christopher and I were inseparable and I supported his cross-dressing. Would you do that for me?

JEFF You want me to lie?

> Arlene rises, reaches for her checkbook and sits confidently again. She writes a check and hands it to JEFF. JEFF'S eyes "pop out" at the amount on the check-which remains in his hand.

VITO Should I call 911?

JEFF There was no sign of life. There's no need to rush. The roads are treacherous. It'll be a while before anybody gets here.

ARLENE Do you approve of the amount?

JEFF (*Looking confused*) What's this for?

ARLENE It's my way of thanking you in advance for the favor you'll be doing to preserve my . . . image.

> ARLENE rises. It's obvious her vivid imagination is in session. She imagines her future Oscar acceptance speech.

ARLENE I thank you all for this honor. Making this film was therapeutic. If I didn't have lines to learn from the brilliant mind of my screenwriter, Jeff Rossi, I would've surrendered to a life of despair. Work was my salvation for my enormous loss-which mothers who've lost a child can relate to. I dedicate this to Christopher. He died of an accidental overdose and not a day goes by that I don't think of him. No mother and son could ever be as close as we were. We loved each other and I love you all.

> VITO applauds but JEFF looks at her incredulously.

JEFF Is that your fictional speech that you plan to deliver?

ARLENE Once your movie receives acclaim for its talented star who-despite her incredible grief, succeeded in delivering an Oscar worthy performance!

JEFF I'm confused. *(Looks at check again)* Is this payment for your future screenplay or is it hush money?

ARLENE I don't like the term "hush money."

JEFF *(Looks at check)* This amount would undoubtedly ensure quality health care for me.

VITO Can I see the check?

    JEFF shows VITO the check he holds.

VITO Holy shit! For that amount I'd do whatever she asks you to do.

JEFF *(Stands)* Arlene, you're not entitled to a free pass just because you have dementia. You can play the sympathy card all you want, but you're still guilty of transphobia. You and for that matter, you too Dad *(looks at VITO)* were brought up in different times when being gay and trans meant breaking the law. *(Alternates looks at ARLENE and VITO)* Fifty years ago people were vilified for their choices. But in these modern times, your comments are unwelcome AND inappropriate. *(Looks only at ARLENE)* Your fans, Arlene, will be shocked to know the real you.

ARLENE What are you saying?

JEFF I don't want to write your screenplay. You're not the person I thought you were.

    VITO begins putting on his coat.

VITO You two need privacy and I need a cigarette break.

ARLENE *(to JEFF)* Do you realize who I am? How dare you refuse to write for me! You have no respect for your elders-nor do you have a sense of luxury. No! *(Sighs)* Loyalty! No sense of loyalty! You asshole! I HATE YOU!!

JEFF Please don't shout at me.

ARLENE Oh, does my temper displease you?

> VITO'S coat and gloves are on as he looks out window.

VITO It stopped snowing.

ARLENE *(to VITO)* You fucking asshole! You're responsible for shattering my son's self-esteem to the point that he took his own life! You're nothing more than a crass, vulgar low-life parasite with a third grade education!

VITO My opinions didn't matter to Christina. What mattered was YOUR opinion. As he wrote in the note, he craved for his mother's approval. He never got it. That was all in the note he wrote.

ARLENE He did NOT write that!

JEFF Yes she did.

VITO That's why you ripped up his note. You don't want anyone to read it 'cause then they'll know you're the villain. *(Beat)* Now, if you'll excuse me, I need some tar and nicotine in my system. Miss Arlene Price: I'm sorry for your loss. What you must feel is something I don't envy. *(to JEFF)* Dinner tomorrow, son?

> JEFF nods as VITO EXITS

ARLENE Did I tell you that I knew Lucille Ball? She was kind and professional. She gave me work on her show-the one with her kids. I remember what a fuss the world made when she gave birth to a boy on the same day that her character, Lucy Ricardo, also gave birth to a boy. *(Laughs)*

> JEFF places ARLENE'S key on her coffee table.

JEFF I have no use anymore for your key.

ARLENE I miss the way life was. In the 1950's the word *pregnant* was unacceptable on TV. If you gave birth to a boy back then, that boy grew up to be a man for his entire life. Not anymore! Pregnant women today can deliver a girl, but there's no guarantee the girl will remain female. She may decide to be a man! *(Laughs)* When did the world get so crazy?

JEFF I better go.

ARLENE Why can't you write for me?

JEFF I won't write scripts for actors that I don't respect. *(Beat)* Actually I could, but not for you. Not anymore.

ARLENE I can't believe my ears!

JEFF Then believe your eyes.

> JEFF rips her last check into shreds.

ARLENE I've written other checks to you. Why haven't you ripped those?

JEFF I've earned every check you've written to me. But no amount can buy my silence. The press and public will know that Christina's death was intentional suicide-not an accidental overdose.

Christina's death won't be in vain. I'm not exposing you for only Christina's sake-although that's reason enough. The public has a right to know the truth. Luckily our public remembers I wrote *Sensitive People* so my credibility won't be questioned. I'm exposing you on behalf of everyone who's been bullied and mistreated for being different. I'm doing it for every non-conformist and-

> JEFF'S cellphone rings-much to ARLENE'S delight.

ARLENE *(sarcastically)* What a shame: your ringing phone interrupted your righteous speech. What a fucking pity!

> JEFF looks at his phone and smiles.

JEFF I don't mind the interruption. Lou wants to reschedule our meeting.

> JEFF finds coat, puts it on and approaches doorway.

ARLENE Will I see you again?

JEFF After I hold a press conference, I doubt you'll want to see me. Luckily the name Arlene Price is a famous one and everyone will be interested in tonight's tragedy. Arlene: I plan to inform the public about how transphobic you really are.

ARLENE You play your part, I'll play mine and we'll see who wins. *(Sighs)* Right now I need you to call the authorities. I want you to report Christina's death as an accidental suicide. Do me that favor. You MUST do that. Is that clear?

JEFF I've got to get out of here.

ARLENE You will not leave while I'm in this

state! I'm unable to cope with this horrendous mess!

JEFF I'm not worried. You have what it takes to survive. I wish your Christina had been born with your survival instincts.

    JEFF opens door, about to make his escape.

ARLENE Don't you dare disclose the contents of Christopher's note! Keep your mouth shut about his suicide! Let them think he died of an ACCIDENTAL overdose. Promise you'll stick to that story.

JEFF I promise nothing.

ARLENE What did I ever do to you?

JEFF It's not what you've done to me, it's what you've done to Christina. Actually it's what you didn't do. You never supported her.

ARLENE Don't leave. I'll pay you to stay! Remember your liver transplant. You need money. That's a fact.

JEFF My integrity comes before my health; I've always been foolish that way.

ARLENE I forbid you to leave!

JEFF I don't know if you're dense or just acting, but I'm no longer your friend. Can you absorb that?

    ARLENE screams; JEFF smiles at her attempt at gaining sympathy.

JEFF Save it for the cameras-should you be so lucky.

    JEFF EXITS.

    ARLENE screams and picks up her cellphone. She ponders how she'll deliver

her lines. She paces as she rehearses her
phone conversation.

ARLENE "Oh, my God, I don't know how I'll
live without my own flesh and blood. He was
everything to me! No mother and son was as
close as Christopher and I. What shall I do
without him? How will I live? All we had
was each other. I can't understand how this
could've happened! How could he have been so
absent-minded-to have taken an accidental pill
overdose? We were more than mother and son.
Christopher considered me his best friend.
I encouraged and supported his dreams, his
choices! Now he's dead from an accidental pill
overdose! Such a shame. What a waste of life.
My baby is gone! Mothers aren't supposed to
bury their kids. I'm heartbroken. This is a
nightmare!"

Arlene screams theatrically and then sits
and dials her cellphone, prepared to
deliver the performance of her life.

Black out

Author's Note

Arlene's Descent was originally performed
without an intermission. I believed that the
play was better served without a break of any
kind, and I have no reason to think otherwise.
However, if an intermission is going to be
used, I would recommend that it come right
before Vito forcing Arlene to admit what she
said before Christina's arrival. The last line
for Act 1 would be:

Christina: Out with it, Ma. *(There's awkward silence. Vito breaks the silence)*
Fade Out
Act 11 would open with Vito's dialogue:
Vito: Your mother said she gave birth to a male. To appease you, she's forced to refer to you as Christina, and she doesn't like doing that.

ARLENE'S DESCENT PROP LIST

Bookcase Grapefruit Juice
Sofa Drinking glasses (4)
Arm Chairs (2) Woman's ornate handbag
Coat rack Pink heeled snow boots
Refrigerator (Visible from adjourning room)
Coffee Table
Vase with red or yellow roses
Bakery cake box
Briefcase
Laptop computer
Manuscript
Cellphones (3)
Mailing Envelopes (4)
Pack of Unopened Cigarettes
Key
Check book
Pen
Folded loose leaf paper (1)
A wet bar
Assorted liquor bottles including:
Bourbon, Whiskey, Vodka
Orange Juice, Cranberry Juice
Ice bucket

SAL ANZALONE was born in the Bronx on July 7th. During his teenage years he lived in the Bronx, Long Island and Brooklyn. "My parents never stayed in one house very long. By the time I made close friends, it was time to move again. Due to unfortunate circumstances, I became an orphan at 21. Since my reality was grim and unpleasant, I manufactured my own-using paper and pen. Writing was always my salvation." It was Anzalone's first play, *Marvin's Fetish* (a Tennessee Williams/New Orleans Literary One-Act Play Finalist) which established him as a playwright. Other plays followed: *Random Outbursts, Unsavory People, Margo's Consent, Jack Best Must Die! Twisted Lucy Fans, Arlene's Descent* and *Straight Seduction.* The subjects explored in Anzalone's plays aren't for the faint of heart. They include sexual obsessions, greed, incest, racism, betrayal, depression and infidelity. His most profound themes, however, are false guilt and loss. His works typically feature gay male protagonists struggling with moral dilemmas. Only two of his plays highlight heterosexual protagonists: *Random Outbursts* and *Jack Best Must Die!* In every work (except *Marvin's Fetish*) you'll find at least one bold and courageous female character who says and does exactly what she pleases and makes no apologies for it.

CASTING STONES

by Alan Baxter

SYNOPSIS

The Reverend Paul Keebler, a minister of a progressive Christian Church in 1968 in Washington, D.C., is caught in a tight dilemma. Located in the ground zero of the riots following Martin Luther King's assassination, Paul must contend with very vociferous protestors, as well as a dysfunctional marriage in his own personal life. Certain conflicts arise quite similar to those which followed George Floyd's murder in 2020.

*A group of actors first did a dramatic reading of **Casting Stones** at a very small Off-Off Broadway theater here in New York City around 2018. Then a reading was done at Trinity Wall Street Church here in New York during a special summer retreat of 2019. Since then there has been more of a demand for this play's production.*

CAST
The Reverend Paul Keebler, a minister of about 28 years
Mary Keebler, his wife of about the same age
Columbine Attwood, a young, free-spirited Hippie activist, early 20's
Samuel McGregor, a very successful Washington executive in his 60's
Leroy Johnson, a young Black activist, in late 20's
Jacques Keroauc, a young Hippie activist, early 20's
Maura Baines, a young Hippie activist, late 20's

CASTING STONES

ACT ONE

SCENE ONE:

The parsonage living room of a relatively old Town House in Washington, D.C., April 4,1968, about 10 blocks east of the Capitol Building. **Mary Keebler**, *an attractive, smart looking woman around 28, dressed in a very conservative outfit, is arranging the flowers on a desk, stage right. Upstage is the front door, and the left of it is an old fireplace, which gives a wonderful, antique charm to the place. Stage right, behind a sofa, is a large bookcase, amply filled, with a small telephone stand next to it. Taped on the walls are signs of the early sixties-----"Power to the People", "Black Power lives On."*
Suddenly the front door opens, and in walks a very distinguished looking man, around 65, who is Mary's father, **Sam McGregor**. *He is dressed in a tailor designed three piece suit.*

    MARY (suddenly turning around)
My God------ (looks) Oh, Dad. You scared me.

    SAM
The place has to be locked. You know I have the key.

    MARY
Paul demands that the doors to this parsonage be opened at all times.

                                SAM
To think, only the most prestigious congressmen
lived in this neighborhood many, many years
ago. Now when I come here, I drive up here in
my beat up Rambler. We're lucky to have a few
Congressmen who at least will show up here on a
few Sundays. We would have more if this were a
better neighborhood.

                               MARY
That's because those distinguished politicians
of yours did not do their job correctly.

                                SAM
I hardly think they were the ones who made this
into a dangerous place.

                               MARY
You know how Paul hates the way you stereo-type
the Southeast.

                                SAM
I firmly agree that Christianity should cater
mostly to the marginalized. That is why I
agreed to Resurrection City at our church, why
I went along with the Marxist library here,
which I'm not so crazy about, and why I agreed
to our donation to the Black Panthers, which
I certainly do not agree with. Sometimes Paul
gets too idealistic.

          (At this point, Paul Keebler walks in from
          Stage Left, from the bedroom. Even though
          he is a minister, his garb would not tell
          you that. With long hair, he is dressed
          in torn blue jeans, wearing an old army

shirt. A tattoo is seen on his left arm.
He is in his late twenties.)

                    MARY
And Paul would tell you that ideals is what
religion is all about.

                    SAM
But there is a point I wish to address him on
in reference to our older kids-----

                    PAUL
And pray God, what should I be telling our
young people about, or what
should I NOT be telling them about. And my
ideals. Have my sermons been heard on deaf
ears.

                    SAM
Good to see you Paul. And let me repeat what
I have been telling you over and over again. I
have been receptive to most of what you have
been preaching. And, as I have been telling
you time and time again, I agree with most of
them. Remember I not only voted for Johnson,
but gave a sizeable donation to his campaign

                    PAUL
And I think I am listening to a broken record
here------

                    SAM
And even though we now have Civil Rights,
the racial injustice and economic disparity
is distasteful. Our American economy can
not grow and become profitable unless we are
a fully integrated society. That is why I

made personal pleas to the Bishop to have you assigned to our church.

              PAUL (hugging his wife)
And you also had a hand in connecting me to this very, very gorgeous woman. (kisses her)

              MARY
There are some things I wanted to talk to you about to buy for Easter. We got to better decorate the Sanctuary for Palm Sunday.

              PAUL
It has to wait until tonight. I have to see Gregory and some of his police buddies at New York Presbyterian. It has to do with housing permits for the National Mall.

              SAM
Actually you are not going to be able to see her tonight-----

     (A surprise pause.)

              PAUL
What the hell-----

              SAM
There is something she doesn't know about yet. There is an important family matter that has to be taken care of.

              MARY
Dad-----

              PAUL
Well, I'm family too. Don't I count? I'm only her husband.

CASTING STONES   150

                              SAM
I'm sorry Paul. I should have told you earlier.
It's my mistake.

                             PAUL
But can't you see that Mary has some important
things to take care of today.

                              SAM
It's just that it's her Aunt Rose. She has to
have her Cancer operation tomorrow. It's been
urgently moved up. I have a business meeting at
the Mayflower Hotel, and she's the only one.

                             PAUL
What do you think about this, Mary.

                              SAM
Paul, I wish that you would------

                             PAUL
Let your daughter speak. It's her decision.

              MARY (after a slight pause)
There are other things we have to decorate for
Easter. That takes time. And Dad, it is very
inconsiderate of you to spring this on me
at the last minute because-----

                              SAM
Mary and I will discuss this-------

                             PAUL
Let her speak for herself, Sam. (pause) I'm fine
with it. However, it's up to you.

MARY (after a lengthy pause)
If you think you can manage, Paul, I do not
want to let Rose down.

(Paul walks over to kiss Mary.)

PAUL
Then have a safe trip. Richmond is not too far
away. I assume you will be gone when I come
back.

SAM
As soon as Rose is out of the hospital, she
will be right back here.

PAUL
Fine, but keep me posted.

MARY
I love you.

SAM
But there is another matter I want to talk
to you about.

PAUL
In a few days. I'm late. I have to be at this
meeting. Oh yeah, Leroy will probably come
by to ask for Columbine. Tell him I have
absolutely no idea where she is. Could be out
of town.

MARY
Fine.

(Paul scurries out the front door.)

SAM

I am sorry, Mary, not to have discussed this with you earlier, but I did not learn of Rose's condition until today. If they break up the lump now, and it is benign, then that will stop the spread.

MARY

I understand, but you know how very busy we are at this time of year, and Paul really wants to be at the forefront of Resurrection City.

SAM

And he shall. Remember I helped him get those Park Permits, and King does have a large staff backing him up.

(Suddenly the front door opens, and two young men and one young woman enter. One young man, **Leroy Johnson**, is African-American, dressed in torn Army fatigues. The other, **Jacques Keroauc**, has on a T-shirt and torn jeans. The woman, **Maura Baines**, wears pleaded shorts.)

JACQUES (waving to Sam)
Up from the Dead?

SAM

That depends on who is alive and who is dead? I am not the Vampire here.

MAURA

Too deep for this hour of the morning

LEROY

What's it with Columbine? Seen her around Mary?

MARY

Come to think of it, I haven't seen her for the
last three weeks. Paul earlier said he didn't
know where she was. He thinks she is out of
town.

LEROY

Nah, she would have told me if she was going
to leave town. I go to the Circle Bar and they
tell me she's not working there for a few weeks

MARY

LeRoy. I think you want her all to yourself.
You're too possessive.

LEROY

Columbine's mind can kinda get really messed
up. She's been tellin' me a lot of stupid ideas
recently. Hope she's not hiding out with JImmy,
that fuckin' pothead. I worry about my woman.

MARY

Now you're getting jealous. That's childish. Go
down to the bar today and maybe she's already
returned.

LEROY

That's cool. We'll check it out. After we wake
up.

        (Sam walks from the fireplace up to where
        Leroy and Jacques are standing.)

SAM

Excuse me, LeRoy and Jacques. I have to ask you
all a dumb question.

JACQUES

You got it, man.

SAM

Sounds like you all just came from the
Sanctuary.

JACQUES

Sure didn't come from the Capitol. We left our
Goldman Sachs and NRA cards home.

LEROY

The Sanctuary is where we all sleep. It's our
barrio.

SAM

But we talked about this at the Trustees
Meeting.

JACQUES

About Resurrection City and The Poor Peoples'
Campaign. And that was approved.

SAM

But that's Resurrection City. No one else. The
sanctuary is not a hotel. One time we came in
for Sunday worship and literally tripped over a
couple having sex in the back pew.

LEROY

That's cool, baby. If it's the House of God,
then it's gotta be the House of Love.

MARY

Leroy, you know that Paul made a resolution
at the Trustees, and you all approved it.

MAURA

But don't you think we as a church are becoming
too litigious ? Look at the growing number of
homeless springing up.

SAM

But we specifically decided that the only ones
sleeping in the sanctuary overnight would be
the participants of Resurrection City----when
they get here.And they are not due here til the
beginning of May.

JACQUES

So we are helping Paul with the part permits
and for sleeping accommodations now, at least
until the Poor People's Campaign gets on its
feet. 3,000 people are supposed to arrive.

SAM

So we'll wait and open the Sanctuary for
sleeping then. That's an order.

MARY

We're doing this to protect our church so
we can be of assistance when King and his
entourage come. Rules have a purpose.

MAURA

No purpose when they cause discomfort to
people.

LEROY (loud and angry)

And that's the shit that's causing everything
in this country to go to hell. Honkies bed down
in their nice suburban homes every night, not
giving a damn about all the filth, poverty, and
crime that goes on in the urban streets.

                    SAM
That's not the point.

                    LEROY
It <u>is</u> the point. If things don't change fast,
Then all the cities in this country will
EXPLODE !!

                    SAM
If we let everyone in the world sleep overnight
in the Sanctuary, and continue to let those
illicit activities continue in the church coffee
house, then we will destroy Ascension Church.
And heavens knows what would be going on there.

                    MAURA
Maybe it's destroyed now.

                    SAM (loud)
That's preposterous. and you know that. I have
worked with Paul to open the door to SNCC,
to the Black Panthers, and to encourage the
continued operation of the Ascension Coffee
House, even though some church members have
heard that there is a lot of profanity and
provocations vented there.

                    LEROY
That's what's it's supposed to be.

                    SAM
As long as it held out in the court yard, then
I encourage it.

                    LEROY
Good. Come down more often.

SAM

When you get rid of the marijuana ! And Paul
lied To me. He said he had stopped all those
activities going on in the Coffee House, and
obviously he hasn't.

MARY

Ok Ok We have to stop this scintillating
discussion. As Dad knows, I have to leave in
the next hour, and Paul is meeting with people
at New York Avenue Presbyterian.

LEROY

I'm good, Sam. Just playin' with ya. I love ya
just the same.

    (Leroy embraces Sam.)

SAM

But please, please try to accommodate us. We do
want to work with you.

    (The three young people start to leave.)

JACQUES

Peace, all.

    (They exit.)

SAM

Paul has to talk with them. In fact, I want to
speak to Paul myself. I am very upset that he
has not been truthful with me.

MARY

You know Paul will work things out.

                              SAM
You always defend him.

                         MARY (angry)
For God's sake, Dad. He's my husband. Although
I wonder if I'm a good enough wife for him.

                              SAM
Stop thinking like that, Mary. There is more to
marriage than just sex.

                             MARY
But I want so much to please him.

                              SAM
You are. You are helping him out tremendously.

                             MARY
Paul gave me the name of a highly recommended
psychiatrist here in D.C. But I told him I did
not want that counseling.

                              SAM
Good. You are giving this matter too much
thought. Paul is a minister, and he ought
to---------

              MARY (getting intensely emotional)
That's right, Dad. He's a minister in an urban
city, right in the ghetto. I want to give him
satisfaction and support when he comes home.
I have seen him walk right in the middle of a
gang fight, where they are attaching each other
with switchblades and guns, trying to calm them
down. I have seen him respectfully argue even
with the police, and I have seen confront the
DC Church Council when they dare to question
the value of our Church.

                          SAM
That's just the point. You seem to think you
have to defend him on everything.

                          MARY
Wait here, Dad. Let me go into the bedroom to
pack a few things. And then we'll be able to
leave.

                          SAM
I will wait for you out in " my locked car."

          (Sam leaves through the front door. Mary
          then starts for the bedroom. Then she
          stops, also realizing there is something
          she should have done. She goes to Paul's
          desk and writes out a short note on one
          of the pads and leaves it for Paul. She
          hesitates for a moment, but then puts the
          note for Paul to see. Then she walks off
          stage into the bedroom as----------)

          (LIGHTS QUICKLY DIM.)

(BLACKOUT)

SCENE TWO

LATER THAT EVENING.

    (SUDDENLY LOUD POLICE SIRENS AND SCREAMS
    ARE HEARD.)

    (An Announcer's Voice in heard in the
    background, against the sound of a frantic
    tele-type machine)

ANNOUNCER:

*We interrupt this program to bring you up to
date news. Martin Luther King has just been
pronounced dead in the Memphis Hospital.
As we announced earlier The Reverend King was
shot down on the balcony right in front of his
motel room in Memphis earlier this evening.
FBI have joined the local police there, and
they hope an arrest will be made very shortly.
Within an hour President Johnson is scheduled
to speak to the nation. We will have that for
you. Stay tuned to WWDC Nighttime Affair..........*

    (LIGHTS COME UP ON KEEBLER'S PARSONAGE.
    It is 11 pm later that evening. All the
    lights are out. FAINT SOUNDS OF STREET
    YELLS ARE HEARD IN THE DISTANCE. Then Paul
    enters through the front door, holding a
    flashlight. He puts it down and then turns
    on the living room lights. He walks into
    the bedroom to check up on something.)

    (PHONE RINGS)

    (Paul walks back into the living room to
    answer it.)

PAUL

Oh, Mary. I'm so glad you called back. I was
worried. I figured you made it there OK………
Did your father make it back To Potomac all
right………………….Yeah, everyone knows now.
I was over at the church a few minutes ago and
everything seems to Be all right…………………….. No,
I think the press are over-reacting.

(SUDDENLY AN EXPLOSION IS HEARD IN THE
DISTANCE.)

………………..But I've locked the door and the
windows are securely shut. ……………………………………………….
Same in the sanctuary……………I don't think
anything will happen………. I'll find out on the TV
later………….I love you too. I'll see you Tuesday.

(Paul hangs up. He then pulls some files
from his lower book case. He then reads
the note that Mary has left him.)

PAUL (muttering to himself)
Off all weekends to be away………….

(Then Paul exits off stage left. A minute
goes by.)

*(Suddenly **Columbine Attwood** rushes in from
the back, a young 20 year old girl, very
animated and wearing an old corduroy shirt
and cut off tight Levi jeans.)*

(Paul enters.)

PAUL
Thank God, it is you. How did you come in?

                    COLUMBINE
     The back door. Don't you ever use it ?

                       PAUL
     But make sure it's locked for tonight.

                    COLUMBINE
     This is crazy, man. Why are they doing this
     shitty stuff. This town's gone crazy. Everything
     we worked for.

                       PAUL
     We all knew it would come to something like
     this.

                    COLUMBINE
     And all the stuff King worked for? Resurrection
     City? What's going to happen to it now?

                       PAUL
     We don't know.

                    COLUMBINE
     Goddamn it. They're gonna destroy themselves.

          (Paul moves closer to comfort Columbine.)

                       PAUL
     Thank God you are all right. I thought I had
     sent you to a hack doctor.

                    COLUMBINE
     No, I'm fine now. Up til last week I still felt
     very sore, but I'm ok now.

                       PAUL
     When did they release you?

COLUMBINE

Two weeks ago. But they let me stay in a
recovery room for two nights. But I just came
back from seeing Leroy.

PAUL

Good. He was looking for you this morning.

COLUMBINE

No. It's not good

PAUL

We told him earlier today that we didn't
know your whereabouts. I didn't want him to
know until it was all over. But he probably
understands now.

COLUMBINE

No, he hates me for it. I told him I went to a
clinic. That made him even angrier.

PAUL

So what does he want you to do? None of you are
in a position to have a child. You know that.

COLUMBINE

His reaction was so unlike him. He scared the
hell out me when he started yelling at me .
Paul, I am starting to feel guilty, really
guilty.

PAUL

Let me get my car and we'll drive to the
Circle.

COLUMBINE

You're crazy. You know what 's going on out
there?

(At this point Columbine pulls Paul over
to her. She touches his hand. Then she
guides Paul's hand overs to her face. Paul
eagerly follows Columbine's direction.
Then she pulls Paul's hand down to her
breasts, and lets him touch her nipples.)

                    COLUMBINE
Finger me . You make me feel so much better.

(Columbine guides Paul's to the area
between her legs to her vagina. Paul
massages it. She then kisses Paul.)

                    COLUMBINE
That feels good, baby. Real good.

(GUN SHOTS ARE HEARD IN THE DISTANCE. WILD
SHOUTING GETS CLOSER. SUDDENLY A MOLOTOV
COCKTAIL IS THROWN.)

                PAUL (urgently)
I've got to go out to stop them.

            COLUMBINE (shouting)
They'll come after you. There's a curfew on.

                    PAUL
No, they won't. They know me

                  COLUMBINE
Stay right here. Isn't the Church locked up?

                    PAUL
They're wouldn't hit it, anyway.

                    COLUMBINE
Where the other guys?

                      PAUL
Stayin' with Brent at the Circle.

      (ANOTHER FIRE EXPLOSION GOES OFF. WILD
      SHOUTING IN THE STREETS. SOUND OF WINDOW
      GLASS BREAKING AND CAR HORNS GOING OFF.)

                    COLUMBINE
Mary all right ? I didn't see her in the
bedroom?

                      PAUL
No, she's down in Richmond.

                  COLUMBINE (angry)
What the fuck is wrong with her? She should be
here to give you support.

                      PAUL
Her aunt is going to have a cancer operation .

                    COLUMBINE
That's her problem. She runs away when disaster
strikes.

                      PAUL
Stop it, Columbine. You know that is not true,
She had no choice.

                    COLUMBINE
 But someone has to be here to help you.

      (SUDDENLY POLICE SIRENS ARE HEARD IN ALL
      DIRECTIONS)

(After looking at each other for a few
seconds, Columbine moves into Paul's arms.
They kiss passionately. Then they stop,
realizing what they have done. Paul then
holds onto Columbine, looking at her in
the eyes.)

PAUL

They're worse off now then when they were
slaves. That's why they have to rebel.

(He then pulls Columbine to him again.)

PAUL

Sometimes we all have to explode, to let the
world know our pain.

(Paul and Columbine continue to kiss
passionately. Then they start to make
love, on the floor in front of the old
fireplace..)

(THE NOISE IN THE STREETS BECOME
EXCRUCIATINGLY LOUD.)

(BLACKOUT)

SCENE THREE

Announcer's Voice in heard in the background, against the sound of a frantic tele-type machine.

ANNOUNCER

"-------*Riots have flared in Detroit, Los Angeles, Milwaukee, and in New York. Mayor Lindsay is now walking the streets of Harlem, greeting many pedestrians of the area, trying to convince them to stay calm. Even here in D.C. violence has gotten way out of hand, and Mayor Washington has summoned the National Guard. But the White House and Capitol have not been touched...........*"

(Lights come up on the Parsonage in the following early morning. The overheard announcer's voice is really the voice on the television, which is now turned towards Paul and Columbine as they now wake up in their blankets. All you see are the flickering lights of the TV.)

(Columbine and Paul have just finished making love. Together they are smoking pot as they *watch the television.)*

COLUMBINE

Turn the damn thing off. It's too early in the morning. There's nothing more we can do now.

(Paul walks over to Stage Left to turn the sound down lower.)

PAUL

At least let me keep the picture on so I know
what is happening. I never thought I would see
army tanks and the National Guard Patrolling
Capitol Hill.

COLUMBINE

That's what we really are. Soon we'll be just
like Spain.

      (Paul crawls back into the blankets and
      rubs his hands across Columbine's body.)

PAUL

Beautiful. You were right. I just needed a warm
pussy.

      (Paul squirms his hands through her legs.)

COLUMBINE (giggling)

Stop. Remember you're a minister.

PAUL (sarcastic)

Yeah, God hates sex.

COLUMBINE

Do you think Mary ever suspects all the nights
we've been having together.

PAUL (still rubbing her vagina)

No. But if she found out, I think she would
understand. She knows what my needs are. But I
gotta hand it to you. You always seem to time
it just right.

COLUMBINE

I never sit next to her in the meetings. But

when she leaves D.C., I take over. She's
either got a woman's Church retreat or some
family member in Richmond.

                    PAUL
Mary thinks I keep the house open at all times
when she is not here. But really I don't. That
shields us. I just tell people I have to have
my Sabbath.

                  COLUMBINE
What's that ?

                    PAUL
A day of rest within the week----given by God.

                  COLUMBINE
Day of rest, bullshit------You closed up to
fuck me. You need someone who knows how to
love you.

                    PAUL
It worked.

                  COLUMBINE
 It's a shame that Mary can't do it.

                    PAUL
Mary can love in her own way. This is the kind
of love she has a hard time understanding.
That is why I know she would understand if she
found out about us.

                  COLUMBINE
When I first camped here at the church, I knew
you were different. Not just because you were
the Pastor, but because you always, always

took responsibility. Your zeal for social
justice was real. Yeah, real for the others,
real for LeRoy. But somehow you never dodged
the bullets. Always so damned stubborn. Always
attacked from both ends, but you always stood
your ground. Your faith in God, your faith in
social justice never seemed to falter.

(Paul gets up to look at the flickering TV
lights and to hear the dimmed sound.)

PAUL
Looks like things have cleared up. The Guard
is letting everyday traffic into the city. Kind
of wish you hadn't toldLeroy I knew about the
abortion. Now he could be coming after me when
he knows you're back in operation.

COLUMBINE
He'll get over it.

(Paul still looks at the TV.)

PAUL
50,000 arrested. That's insane. Where are they
Putting them?

COLUMBINE
Goddamn police state (agitated) First they kill
King, now they'restarting to rub out a lot of
us.

PAUL
That's how it gets started. The police over-
react, they shoot down a couple of looters,
then what was a small scuffle becomes a riot.

                    COLUMBINE
Shit for all of us.

        (Again, Paul looks closely at the TV)

                      PAUL
Great news.

                    COLUMBINE
What's that.

                      PAUL
Abernathy's taking over King's position. He's
going to head up Resurrection City and bring
them to DC.

                    COLUMBINE
Hope the city is ready for them now.

        (Paul walks over to the front window, next
        to the front door, and pulls away the
        curtain.)

                      PAUL
Yeah, things have quieted down now. I haven't
heard too many sirens in the last four hours.
It's probably safe to go out.

                    COLUMBINE
Be careful.

                      PAUL
I want to check the Sanctuary. There still
might be a curfew tonight.

                    COLUMBINE
Let the fuckin' pigs do it. It's their job.
Come back to bed.

(Paul then snuggles back under the blanket
with Columbine.)

                    PAUL
For a peacenik, you're starting to sound very
militaristic.

                  COLUMBINE
You gotta be resilient to fight those fuckers in
the White House. You know how many bombs and
poison gases our planes are dropping on Viet
Nam every day. The way they are destroying the
earth is fuckin' terrible.

          PAUL (touching her again)
But that's why I could never stop loving
you----

                  COLUMBINE
I've told you about my stupid father--- my dada

                    PAUL
Not again----

                  COLUMBINE
As Vice-President of Coca-Cola, he made a lot
of goddamn money. He even purchased this summer
home on one of the islands not too far from the
Florida Everglades. Out in the middle of
nowhere where we wouldn't get into trouble.
A slab of luxury surrounded by some of the
poverty and desolation of the world. I hated
the fact that Dad made so much fuckin' dough.

        (LOCAL STREET SCREAMING IN THE
        BACKGROUND.)

                    PAUL
Yeah, tell me you wished you were there
now-----

                  COLUMBINE
My old man insisted we spend the summer there,
especially when I was in high school. But on
certain nights, I would sneak out to the beach
and sleep out there all night, naked under the
stars. That was really a trip.

                    PAUL
I wouldn't recommend that in front of the
Capitol building. Or, on second thought, maybe
that would work.

        (Columbine gets up and walks to the
        window)

                  COLUMBINE
But out in the middle of nowhere, it could also
get real chilly in the early morning. But it
was amazing how damp your clothes were when
you woke up in the almost dark morning. The
moisture in the air soaked right into your skin
and you became drenched with humidity. But that
sun coming up over the ocean made me feel so
much warmer, and so pure. That is partly how I
feel having you inside me. But that miraculous,
warm sun.

                    PAUL
Like what Aton does to us frail humans.

                  COLUMBINE
Who is Aton?

                              PAUL
The name of Akhenaton's God. Visualized in the
sun

                            COLUMBINE
Akhenaton?

                              PAUL
A famous Egyptian Pharaoh who believed in
monotheism almost two hundred years before
Moses. Maybe it was Aton who really spoke to
Moses. Aton, Jehovah, Father, Brahman, Allah---
--different names for the same God.

                            COLUMBINE
Then you're not a Christian.

                              PAUL
Oh, I definitely am ! Maybe the DC Church
Council does not think I am, but I really do
believe in what Jesus of Nazareth taught. Is
just that God transcends names.

                            COLUMBINE
What caused you to become a preacher ?

                              PAUL
I became a preacher as a result of a bet !

                            COLUMBINE
A bet. That's wild !

                              PAUL
A couple of buddies and me-----We got together
a year after We graduated from Wilson High here
in DC. We were kinda stoned. But all we knew

back then was that all we wanted to go into was
some kind of field—some career---that would help
humanity. Altruism, you might say. So we all
drew straws, each with a different career.

                    COLUMBINE
Crazy.

                    PAUL
One would be becoming a lawyer, another a
doctor, another a social worker, and another
a minister. We didn't know which was which. We
took bets on the numbers.

                    COLUMBINE
So the straw you ended up with was the
minister.

                    PAUL
You got it. So I enrolled at Howard University.
Was the only White student In my class. Then
continued on in their religious seminary,
graduated------ And here I am.

                    COLUMBINE
So you think you lost the bet?

                    PAUL
No. I won.

                    COLUMBINE
With all these problems-----

                    PAUL
With all these problems, I have had a chance to
help establish what I think is God's demands.

COLUMBINE

I don't get you, baby. What God demands ?

PAUL

What I think God wants us to have. I think God
wants all of us to have an equal piece of the
pie. In God's economy, it's not who gets in
to the end goal first, not who gets to reap the
biggest profit, and not who has to be the lowest
paid worker. God wants everyone to be equally
fulfilled. And no one gets in first or no one
gets in last. As long as no one is left behind.
That's the sum of Jesus of Nazareth's teachings.

    (Columbine walks back to Paul and nestles
    under the blanket with him)

COLUMBINE

With everything that's going on, do you still
believe in God ?

PAUL

I believe in God, more now. We're all going to
have dark days, growing pains, but eventually
God leads us to a solution. When I see a racist
hug a person of color and help him out in
whatever way he can, then I know that God is
real. When I see our more well off volunteers
from the church, sacrifice their time in our
soup kitchen, then I know God is very close
to us. When I see young draft dodgers put
their careers on the line and when I see young
South American liberation priests put their
lives on the line to eradicate the poverty and
oppression of the hard-working, then I know God
is Real.peasant and farmer, then I definitely
know that God is within us all.

COLUMBINE

Super.

    PAUL (kneels to touch her breasts)
And your marvelous energy and super beauty, as
well as Mary's love, is also apartial window of
the Divine in my life. You've been my Guardian
Angel these past 48 hours.

    (Paul then kisses Columbine again very
    passionately.)

               PAUL

I love you .

    (SUDDENLY MARY WALKS ABRUPTLY THROUGH THE
    FRONT DOOR.)

               MARY

Paul----are you here?

(BLACKOUT)

ACT TWO

SCENE ONE

Ascension Church, five days later. The Parsonage.
Later in the afternoon. The parsonage now seems
very peaceful, compared to the prior evenings.
The broken window has been repaired. However,
there are no longer blankets in front of the
fireplace.

(Suddenly Columbine enters from the back.
She has on a jacket and some long legged
blue jeans, and is carrying a back pack.
She puts it down near the desk, looks
around the living room, and walks out into
the kitchen.)

(Then Mary enters the front door, very
quietly. She slowly puts her purse on
the desk. Then she notices the back pack
near the desk, and then figures out who it
possibly must belong to. Mary then walks
over to examine the repaired window. Then
she slowly sits down on the sofa.)

(Then Columbine suddenly enters from the
kitchen.)

OLUMBINE
Mary-----what a surprise.

MARY (sarcastic)
I guess one should be surprised. It must beOdd
seeing a wife sitting in her own home. strange
to see the wife in her own house.

COLUMBINE

After you arrived that night, Paul and I wanted
to talk with you.

MARY (still sarcastic)

That's strange. But you would not have been
able to. My uncle was waiting outside in the
car.

COLUMBINE

Mary, I know how you must feel. We're very
sorry. We can explain.

MARY (angry)

Please be truthful. That's not you Columbine.
But what can you say after all these days when
you and Paul were lying to me. That's pretty
cowardly, don't you think ? Cheating on me
behind my back. And now when I am away, you
practically squatter inside my home, rob me of
my role as a wife, and make love to a man I
have spent many years supporting and building
up so he could face the perils of inner city
struggles.

COLUMBINE

You make it sound like Paul is the only one who
has to put up with ghetto existence. You think
being faithful is to desert him the nightshe
needed you the most.

MARY

My aunt needed me.

COLUMBINE

No, your father needed you. You know, you are
very outdated . Family tradition is not nearly

as important as fighting the fascism of our society.

MARY

And being indifferent to family struggles---is not that a wrongful attitude.

COLUMBINE

You're just parroting the junk your father has told you.

MARY

That's incorrect, and Paul knows it. And I disagree many times with what my father says, and you're probably using that false reasoning with my father in order to justify an excuse for convincing my husband to cheat on me.

COLUMBINE

Paul and I were not cheating on you. I was simply giving Paul the love you were incapable of giving him. And up to now, he was thankful of your supportive feelings. Now things have changed.

(Paul suddenly enters the parsonage through the front door.)

PAUL

Mary, I have been trying to reach you.

MARY

Maybe you and Columbine can tell me what has changed. I suppose Columbine is now the First Lady of the Church.

PAUL

I don't know what Columbine is talking
about, but I really want to have a moment by
ourselves, so we can talk this out. Hiding
yourself from me is not the answer.

MARY

You accuse me of hiding. Haven't you been
hiding from me as you play these sexual games
of unfaithfulness behind my back.

PAUL

That is not true. You put everything out of
perspective, and then you spread stories that
exaggerate the truth.

COLUMBINE

We had our talk, Paul, and I tried to convince
her otherwise.

MARY

I will excuse myself to the bedroom, where I
have to get my things together before Emily
picks me up.

PAUL

Mary, you have not given me the chance. I would
like to think we could talk it out to see what
went wrong. A few nights ago you ran out of
here before------

COLUMBINE

Goddamnit, Mary, listen.

(Mary then pulls away from most of them)

MARY (angry)
So what are you people? What would any woman do
when her husband has lied to her over the last
month. To hell with both of you. Are you so
blind you don't care how you have hurt me !!

COLUMBINE:
Listen, please------

PAUL
Columbine, let her alone so she can speak her
mind.

COLUMBINE
But I have to say something to Paul.

MARY
Go ahead. I need to go to the bedroom to get
more of my things.

(Paul goes over to Mary to try to comfort
her, and puts his arm on her shoulder.)

PAUL
Mary, I would like to--------

MARY (crying)
Get your damn hands off me.

(Mary then exits. Then a pause)

PAUL
She is in pain, and I well understand why.

(Columbine then walks to the other side of
the living room in wild gestures.)

                        COLUMBINE
But we're all in pain over what has happened.
King is dead, and much of what we have worked
for is dead.

                          PAUL
That's not true. Resurrection City is still
going to happen, and they're still coming to
Washington, and I want to be here to help them.

                        COLUMBINE
If those fuckers allow you to stay here-----

                          PAUL
No, I will talk to them. I am their minister.
They will let me stay. People were scared away
these last few days, but they will be back.
Jim andKeith did come by to help me repair a
few things in the sanctuary, and we still will
be able to have our Coffee House and we will be
able to celebrate Easter this Sunday.

                        COLUMBINE
You hope------

                          PAUL
But I was really worried about you Columbine.
Where were you these last Few days?

        (Columbine approaches Paul. They start to
        touch each other again.)

                        COLUMBINE
I shacked up with Jaime. He needed me. He's
all fucked up. You know where he lives at the
Circle. Very close to Leroy.

PAUL

In a situation like this, that is the last
place you should Have gone to.

COLUMBINE

Where else could I have stayed with Mary having
discovered us.

PAUL

She is just frightened at what she saw. We did
nothing wrong. I was hoping we could talk it
out.

COLUMBINE

I'm sorry. I should have tried to get back to
you. But how? Mary could have picked up the
phone. I did not know she had gone.

PAUL

You're spending too much time with Jaime. It's
dangerous. You know he's a speed freak.

COLUMBINE (shouting)

Why make such a big deal about it-----

(Paul lovingly embraces Columbine.)

PAUL

I'm just worried about you. Don't get so
personal. It's just that I need you here !

(Columbine walks over to where the
fireplace is and slowly picks up her
knapsack.)

COLUMBINE

Paul, we're leaving.

                    PAUL (shocked)
Leaving? Where?

                    COLUMBINE
Maybe upstate New York, Vermont, Michigan----
Who knows.

        (Just at that moment Leroy enters through
        the front door. Columbine puts down her
        knapsack.)

                    PAUL
But you know I need you here to help me. And
what do you Mean by "we" ?

                    LEROY
She also means "me", man.

                    PAUL
Leroy !!

        (At this point, Leroy walks over and puts
        his arm around Columbine.)

                    LEROY
We made up. I deeply apologized to her for what
I did wrong.

        (He kisses her at this point.)

                    LEROY
And if you want, you can apologize to me.

                    PAUL
Apologize to you. But why? I was not trying to
steal her away from you. I was not trying to be
a better sexual partner.

CASTING STONES   186

                    COLUMBINE (persistent)
I kept telling you, Leroy. Paul was the only
one I could talk to.

                         PAUL
She was lost, Leroy. And guilt ridden.

                    LEROY (angry)
But you forget somethin', man. She's <u>my</u> woman.

                         PAUL
"My woman." You make it sound like you possess
her. You don't own her.

                         LEROY
Fuck you, man. Where the hell you get off
telling the Black Man what he can or can not
own.

                         PAUL
Leroy------

        (Leroy walks over and directly confronts
        Paul.)

                    LEROY (very angry)
Ever since the Black Man walked the earth
of this goddamn country, he's never owned
anything. Instead everyone tried to "own
him."-----own his body by forcing him into
slave labor------own his soul by telling us
we weren't as pure and as righteous as you
supposedly are.

                       COLUMBINE
Leroy, you know Paul is not saying that.

LEROY (loud and angry)
What the hell you think all this street violence
has been all about? Because of what they did to
Dr. King? Yeah, that's part of it. But a hell
of a lot more. They just couldn't take it any
longer.. No career jobs for the Black Man----We
don't want you in the suburbs, so we're going
to keep you in the ghetto------where you're
going to pay more for your groceries, where the
schools are all damn lousy, where the public
services don't give a shit about you, where the
police pigs are always following you, and where
you'll always be at the mercy of the Mafioso drug
dealers. That's why we're fighting back.

(Paul starts to walk away from Leroy.)

PAUL
And you're giving me a lecture on something I
know nothing about?

LEROY
And the white man tells us we're just predatory
male animals ? They have a hell of a lot of a
nerve to tell us that after watching the stunt
that you pulled and which the whole church
knows about now.

PAUL
Leroy, how can you associate me with such
racism?

COLUMBINE
He doesn't mean it that way, Paul.

PAUL (very angry)
Leroy, we've been like brothers. How many times

have we gone to Capitol Hill to drive some
sense Into those narrow-minded Congressmen. How
many times have we dodged tear gas bombs in
Mississippi, Georgia. Count The number of times
we got arrested in Virginia, Alabama. How can
you accuse me of this racism?

(Leroy confronts Paul right in his face.)

LEROY
It's just that Columbine aborted my child--
-a child that I did give her. And you lied to
me about it. (more intense) And you know you
would be damn mad if that were your own child.
You knew all about it, and didn't have the
decency to tell me. And instead, she winds up
in bed with you.

PAUL (very defensive)
I know…..I know you have every right to be
very angry. And I'm sorry. I'm sorry. I just
had to give her comfort. And you couldn't.
You tried to beat her up that night. So where
was she supposed to go? So It just happened…..
nature got the best of us…….and it shouldn't
have.

(Paul looks Leroy right in the eye.)

PAUL
And I promise you. It will never, never happen
again.

(Leroy moves away from Paul. Then there
is a long pause. Then he moves straight
up to Paul.)

                    LEROY
Just wanted to hear those words from you.

        (Leroy puts out his hand to Paul.)

                    LEROY
Put it there man. We're good.

        (Columbine goes to embrace Paul)

                  COLUMBINE
Paul, we never stopped loving you.

                    LEROY
So, Paul------ we want you to come with us.

        (Paul is somewhat shocked.)

                    PAUL
But I got to stay here and help with The Poor
People's Campaign. At the Church, we have to
let the media know what this is all about.

                  COLUMBINE
But you can't do it at this Church. They won't
let you. After what Mary discovered, they will
never let you stay a minister here.

                    LEROY
Come with us, man.

        (There is a long pause here.)

                    PAUL
I can't. Even if I am not in the church, I can
still help Abernathy here in Washington. And
more important, I need to stay with Mary.

COLUMBINE (shocked)
Paul, you're stupid. You heard what she feels about you. You're crazy.

PAUL
But I did hurt her.

COLUMBINE (loudly)
But she's like a spoiled child. As soon as she saw me in bed with you, she blabbed about it to everyone else in the church. And look at her old man. They're establishment.

PAUL
Things like that don't matter. Whatever new job I take, I will try to be here in Washington with her. It means everything to her.

COLUMBINE
Unfortunately, it means everything if you give in to Mary and her father. By doing that, you are going against what we both stand for and turning your backs on your beliefs as well.

PAUL
Hurting a person's feelings !! That certainly is a part of my beliefs as well.

(Columbine and Leroy nod to each other. Then Columbine goes up to Paul.)

COLUMBINE
Just like I told you, you're too fuckin' stubborn.

(There is a pause. Then Leroy embraces Paul.)

                         LEROY
That's ok, man. We understand.

                         PAUL
I don't think you do.

                       COLUMBINE
What difference does it make. Whatever you did,
I got a feeling you'll make it right.

     (Paul embraces Columbine very intensely. A
     long pause.)
                         PAUL
I wish I could convince you to stay. But I
never, never will forget you.

     (Columbine kisses Paul_

                       COLUMBINE
Thanks for your support.

     (Both Leroy and Columbine open the front
     door and leave the parsonage. However,
     Columbine has left her back pack near the
     fireplace. There is a few minutes pause.
     Paul goes over to his desk and pulls out
     his small glass of whiskey to settle his
     nerves.)

     (Then Mary enters from the bedroom upstage
     left, with one of her suitcases packed.)

                         MARY
Paul, you are all alone?

     (After a beat, Paul slowly looks over.)

PAUL

Leroy and Columbine left for good. Probably both you and I will never see them again.

MARY

Leroy, here ?

(Paul still stands a bit aloof.)

PAUL

You didn't hear him? And you're not the only one. He raked me over the coals as well. And now --- now we're all alone.This should relieve you of any fears that you might have that I was planning to dump you and run away with them.

MARY (after a pause)

I understand, Paul.

PAUL

I know the whole Church knows. Don't you think we could have talked it out before you told everyone about Columbine and myself.

(Mary sits down on the couch. There is a pause.)

MARY (almost crying)

I was frightened, Paul. You can't imagine how shocked I was to see you with her in bed. Those things I can't handle. I'm sorry.

(Paul looks over to Mary.)

PAUL

Mary, you of all people do not have to apologize. From what I've heard this past week, there are some out to tar and feather me

                    MARY
I don't know why people have to use you as the
scapegoat.

          (Paul starts to walk over to the group of
          books he has on his desk. He opens his
          Bible, turns and fumbles around for the
          exact passage he was looking for.)

          (There is a pause.)

          PAUL (mumbling to himself as he reads)
"Why have you despised the word of the Lord,
To do what is evil in his sight……….."

                    MARY
Paul, you were never so adamant about reading
the Bible out loud.

                    PAUL
I always thought that Christianity was
greater than just a book.

                    MARY
What are you reading?

                    PAUL
2 Samuel, Chapter 12

                    MARY
Paul, you don't have to be so hard on
yourself. David allowed a man to be killed.
You didn't.

                    PAUL
But look how I hurt you------

                    MARY

You have to understand how I felt then.
to feel abandoned by your own husband-----

                    PAUL

But that is where I went so wrong.

        (A slight pause. Mary gets up and walks a
        few steps away, over to the window.)

                    MARY

I was probably too dependent on you and my
father, so I was not able to decide for myself
what my own direction should be. Maybe that is
the good that came out of this. We have to know
ourselves better, and God willing, to be able
to face the crazy events of this life. You have
said it. We have to look at the whole picture,
not get buried in one isolated incident.

        (She turns around and walks towards Paul.)

                    MARY

I know you are sorry for your mistake.

                    PAUL

Why don't people realize that as ministers we
are human as well. We can't go about acting as
models of perfection.Who can? We have needs as
anyone else.

        (Mary starts to leave.)

                    PAUL

Would you please give me another chance to be
honest with you.

(There is a short pause.)

MARY

Paul, I have thought it over. Maybe I should
see that therapist you mentioned. (pause) I
realize I never did my part to help fulfill
you.

PAUL

Whatever you want.

MARY

I am sure the Church Council, my Father, and
many other regular members will want you to
resign as Pastor of Ascension Church. I know
you don't want me to mention this, but my
Father said he would help you. He's going to
talk to the Bishop. He's going to ask him to
let you keep your pension, for the future when
you need it. Father thinks he can get you a job
in social work, and he will pull some strings
for you. It would be in another state, so you
can leave Washington. I don't think I liked
being a minister's wife anyway.

PAUL

So you will stay with me ?

MARY

You will let me ?

PAUL

Yes, why not.

MARY

But we will probably have to leave Ascension
and leave Washington.

(Paul walks around the room.)

PAUL

I understand. But social justice programs, the
Coffee House, the Poor People's Campaign----what
will happen to them ?

MARY

They will probably dismantle and be no more, at
least not in this Church. The "older regulars"
are all upset over the violence that took place
a number of days ago.

PAUL

I see.

MARY

But if you confess to the whole Church this
Easter Sunday morning that you were wrong in
your actions, then I am sure they will support
youin your new transition in life.

PAUL (after a short pause)

Of course, I will agree to it. I don't think I
have any choice. Again, what will you do ?

MARY

I am still confused. My nice, comfortable world
has flipped twice over the last few days, so
I can't decide now. I am still staying with
Emily, but I will definitely see you Easter
morning.

(Mary goes over to give Paul a short
kiss.)

                              MARY
Good-bye.

        (Mary picks up her other suitcase and
        leaves through the front door. Again Paul
        is left alone in the house. He takes
        another glass of whisky, and then sits
        down to think, and probably even to pray.)

        (Minutes go by in his solitude. Then he
        looks over and eyes the backpack Columbine
        had left. He walks over to pick it up,
        thinks for a moment, then walks over to
        the bedroom with more determination.)

(BLACKOUT)

SCENE TWO

Easter morning at the same parsonage. It is brightly lit with some new vases filled with bright lilies. Maura enters with another vase of flowers and puts them on the fireplace. She then attempts to add a finishing touch to the Living room.

> (Paul enters. He is dressed up in a bright 3-piece suit.)

PAUL

Maura, you're here early.

MAURA

Easter morning. I promised you I would have the Sanctuary looking good.

PAUL

I saw it. It looks good. With all the violence quieted, we probably will have a good crowd.

MAURA

There's this one cop who insists on standing security in the front narthex. If they had their way, they would change our church to a fuckin' prison.

PAUL

That's ok. It's probably Johnnie. He's a rookie on the force. But a really good one.

> (Maura then walks over to straighten Paul's tie. She is nervous, along with Paul.)

                    MAURA
Good luck today, Paul.

        (They quickly embrace.)

                    PAUL
Say three prayers for me……no, make it six.

        (Immediately, Sam McGregor lets himself
        in. Maura then exits.)

                    MAURA
See ya later Sam

                    SAM
You're early.

                    PAUL
So are you.

        (Sam walks over to shake his hand.)

                    SAM
Happy Easter. I think things will work out. I
know they will. Have you seen Mary?

                    PAUL
She's with Emily. She said she would be here
today.

                    SAM
I think we should sit together when you're
addressing the congregation.

                    PAUL (sarcastic)
Strange you should say that.

                    SAM
Also, the Bishop wants you to fill out some
paperwork.He said he would also send in a
recommendation for your other job. And I think
you will like it.

     (There is a short pause.)

                    PAUL
But all that will not be necessary.

     (Sam is startled.)

                    SAM
I'm sorry. What did you say?

                    PAUL
I said it would not be necessary. Sam I am not
resigning as Minister of this parish. I am
staying on.

                    SAM
But Mary said you were leaving the Church and
leaving the ministry.

                    PAUL
That was a few days ago. Today I have decided
differently. I am not resigning.

                    SAM
Does Mary know.

                    PAUL
She will when she gets here

                    SAM
Paul, I can not believe I am hearing this. You

don't have a choice. Many of your followers have left, and the regulars want you out so the Church can move on. In fact, you have been an embarrassment to this Diocese. All your lies and your deceptive practices-----

PAUL
There will be only truth said this morning from the pulpit.

SAM (angry and loud)
How can you say that to the congregation when you have lied both to me and to Mary. You are going to address everyone today---young kids, families, well-to-do senior citizens, and even some politicians, and admit you were an irresponsible husband—an adulterer? Don't you think you were wrong in what you did?

(Paul walks over to the other side of the living room, then turns over to Sam.)

PAUL
Wrong? You think I was wrong in what I particularly did? (pause) Don't we all do "wrong" everyday in our lives. Sam, have you ever in your life had to tell a white lie to someone—or to all of us---everyday of our lives? We do wrong every working day. We probably do wrong when we dip in our forks and eat the flesh of an animal who has been tortured in some slaughter house. We do wrong when we buy that beautiful brand new shirt made by the gnarled hands of an over-worked, under-paid factory worker in some under-developed Third World Country. Or we do wrong when we let the State seize young men, hand them an assault

weapon, and order them to kill other human
beings different from them.

                    SAM
So you are going to tell the entire
congregation this morning that you were
justified in cheating on your wife --- my
daughter?

                    PAUL
Yes.

                    SAM
You're out of your mind.

                    PAUL
Yes, God willing, I am going to defend myself,
and I do not think I was, as you put it,
"cheating" on her. All three of us, Mary,
Columbine, and myself had special needs we had
to fulfill.

                    SAM
And to fulfill your particular needs, you had to
break a marital oath---You had to be unfaithful
to my daughter, your wife? You think God wanted
you to do that?

                    PAUL
There are many times when it is hard to figure
out what God wants. But there are times when we
have to break rigid moral laws to achieve
what God does want us to do.

                    SAM
That is some idiotic theology you have. There
are some God given moral laws and "strict"

rules, as you put it, that we have to obey. And when we don't, we have "hell" to pay. Civilized society can not exist without a sense of order. And look at what has been happening the last few days !! And respect for your wife is part of that order. And you endorse disorder?

PAUL
No, Sam, I do not. You know that. But there are growing pains and frustrations we have to go through. But at the end, we arrive at a greater compassion for our fellow man. And that "compassion", not blind obedience to traditional social morality, is what God wants from all of us.

(At this point Sam walks up the stairs to exit.)

SAM
Paul, you articulate things very well, but you will fail to succeed in what ministerial career you think you have, and your little justification speech this morning will only under mind what the Church and society have tried to promote.

PAUL
Resurrection City and the Poor People's Campaign is trying to resolve the social economic needs of this city, Washington, and of this entire country. And I will continue struggling to have the church involved in that process.

(Sam walks up to the front door.)

                    SAM (very angry)
I will never support you, nor do I think
the church will keep you as their minister,
especially after the little stunt you pulled.
But, if Mary decides to stay with you, I will
support what little marriage you think you
have. But I will not lift a finger, nor give
you money, nor recommend you for whatever else
you want to do in life.

                    PAUL
Somehow, Sam, I would be suspicious of your
support anyway. You're afraid of life and
you've imposed your fear of life on Mary.
That's why you hold her hostage to you.
You've lost a lot of your loving humanity,
and now you're trying to drain it from Mary.
That's your problem. You keep trying to
control people and you're too frightened by
change.

        (Before Sam opens the door to leave, he
        turns back.)

                    SAM
But we can't change unless we have some moral
direction, some model. and that is something
you cannot give us. (pause) Good-bye, Paul.

        (At this moment Mary walks into the living
        room, from the kitchen. Paul turns around
        and is surprised when he sees her. She is
        dressed in a very pretty spring outfit.)

                    PAUL
You were in the bedroom all this time?

MARY

The backdoor. We hardly ever use it.

PAUL

So you overheard everything?

MARY

Most of it

PAUL (pause)

I'm sorry I had to speak to your father that
way.

MARY

He will get over it. He really does still love
us, I know. He has to learn to listen to other
people's opinions more. I am sure he will not
leave you out in the cold and will help you in
some way.

PAUL

It's all in God's hands.

MARY

I am learning to dispute with him more. But I
realize now that returning to him or agreeing
with him would not make me in the least bit
happy.

PAUL

If you're willing to stay with me, it might
turn out to be very tough. I might lose out
this morning. Certainly no future pension and
no income for awhile.

MARY

I told you my world had flipped a couple of

times. I just need time to think. Emily says I
can stay with her.

                    PAUL
You need time. I cannot deny you that.

                    MARY
If you lose, you'll just have to find a new way.
I have signed up for teaching next year. You
might find a good social work job. There are
other churches that I am sure will want you.
You might not even need me.

        (There is a long pause. Then Paul walks
        over to Mary and holds her .)

             PAUL (crying a bit)
I'm----I'm really sorry I hurt you. I am also
sorry for not seeing you as you really are.

                    MARY
Maybe it is my deep love for you that makes me
forgive you. Most women wouldn't. You
wouldthink I had more pride.

                    PAUL
Don't ever say that !

        (Mary then gives a short kiss to Paul.)

                    MARY
It was I who never really appreciated the love
you were trying to give me. I also just did not
care enough about your situation. I saw it the
wrong way. (pause) But I think I now have the
strength to work it out. But still let's live
separately for a while

PAUL

Remember, we are seeing that counselor
together. I want to be there with you.

MARY

It will work out.

PAUL

I have no idea what the future holds for us.

MARY

Whatever happens, we'll persevere. Because you
stuck to your beliefs.

    (At this point Paul and Mary embrace.)

PAUL

You just might have to learn to trust me when
we can sleep together again, I hope.

MARY

I panic so much when that moment comes. I used
to have these nightmarish feelings when that
moment came.

PAUL

Believe me. I am not trying to harm you. Trust
in me more if that moment comes again.

    (They start to passionately kiss each
    other. Then there is a pause.)

MARY

 I love you.

PAUL

You know Einstein's quote: (mimicking) "I

CASTING STONES   208

do not think God would play dice with the universe." (himself) But I think God *does* play dice with us humans. And to tell you the truth, I have learned to love it.

                    MARY
Let's be positive. Maybe the Church this
morning will support you and let you continue
to be their minister. We'll just have to see.
For better or for worse.

                    PAUL
For better or for worst.

                    MARY
Scary words.

                    PAUL
Very scary words.

                    MARY
It's Easter. That's all that matters.

          (Both Mary and Paul move up the stairs to
          leave, as the CHURCH BELLS CHIME.)

(BLACKOUT)

                    THE END

PROP LIST

One 1960's Black and White TV Set, with antennas
A woman's elegant overcoat
One 1960's Radio
One pad of paper
One box of envelopes
One packet of marijuana
Two suitcases
One Church Bulletin
Two sets of Keyes
One Dial-up Telephone
Three backpacks
Some hard cover books, such as Das Kapital, Malcolm X, Native Son, etc.
A Bible
3 vases of Easter flowers (lilies)
One Pot of Coffee
Two coffee cups
A portable typewriter
Two large blankets
One brick

Having been a mainstay of the New York City Poetry Circuit for the last twenty years, Alan Baxter has read as a featured poet at Evie Ivy's Dance of the Word, the Bowery Poetry Club, ABC No Rio, The Green Pavilion, and The Brownstone Poets. He has had his poems published in the following anthologies: *Dinner with the Muse, Nomad's Choir* and *The Venetian Hour*. He hosted the Kairos Poetry Café in Manhattan for almost eighteen years, and in 2010 published his first book of poetry *Shall We Have Magic?* His other book *A Second of Eternity* has just been released. He now assists Chester Johnson with the poetry program at Trinity Wall Street Church in New York City, as well as reading poetry at St. Johns and at The Church of the Village in Greenwich Village.

Alan Baxter is not only a film-maker who has co-produced many independent movies, but he is also the founder of AB Film Productions, which a number of years ago mounted the award winning film *Barriers*, which Mr. Baxter personally directed. He is also the producer of the documentary *Artwatch* which contains interviews with leading art historians who have appeared many times on the famous TV show *60 Minutes* Mr. Baxter also wrote the play *Juan and Emmett* which Ivy Theatre produced in a small theater in New York City. He also co-produced the documentary feature The *New Patriots*, still showing on Amazon Prime Video, and this spring he hopefully will be able to release his newly directed film *Exhorter*.

Professor Baxter has taught literature and basic writing at The College of New Rochelle and at Ramapo College. He was brought up in Silver Spring, Maryland, right outside Washington, DC, and later graduated from The College of William and Mary and did his graduate work at American University. Now he lives in both Greenwich Village, New York City and in Montreal, Canada.